BACK ROADS LORE

STRANGE HARVEST

LEWIS - WEATHERLY - NELSON

Published by

EERIE LIGHTS

Eerie Lights Publishing

BACK ROADS LORE VOLUME 4 STRANGE HARVEST

BY LEWIS - WEATHERLY - NELSON

Based on travel, interviews, and research conducted by Back Roads Lore.

ISBN: 978-1-945950-53-7

Published by Eerie Lights Publishing

Cover Art by Shawn Engelmann

Editor: Jerry Hajewski

Layout | Design: Digital Cricket Designs
DigitalCricketDesigns@proton.me

Printed in the United States of America

Back Roads Lore
backroadslore.com

EERIE LIGHTS

eerielights.com

eerielightspublishing.com

TABLE OF CONTENTS

Features

Columns

Introduction

As you can probably guess, we at Back Roads Lore love the Autumn season and all the things it brings—crisp leaves, a chill in the air, and people in the mood for spooky things—it's just the kind of atmosphere that suits us!

We considered a lot of various options for this volume, but we decided to focus on the season itself and its rich traditions, so we're presenting you with a deep dive into topics you might think you know a lot about—but maybe you don't.

David delves into the origins of the jack-o'-lantern, Kevin explores the lore of scarecrows, and Chad takes a look at tainted Halloween candy—are those treats in your bag really safe?

Bats, ghouls, graveyard monsters, melonheads—they're all here as well as much more. Our regular columns offer seasonal fare as well with pieces about the Halloween capital of the world, an Edgar Allan Poe Museum and much more.

We hope you enjoy the seasonal bonfires, pumpkin patches, and haunted house visits, and, of course, Back Roads Lore!

Back Roads Lore

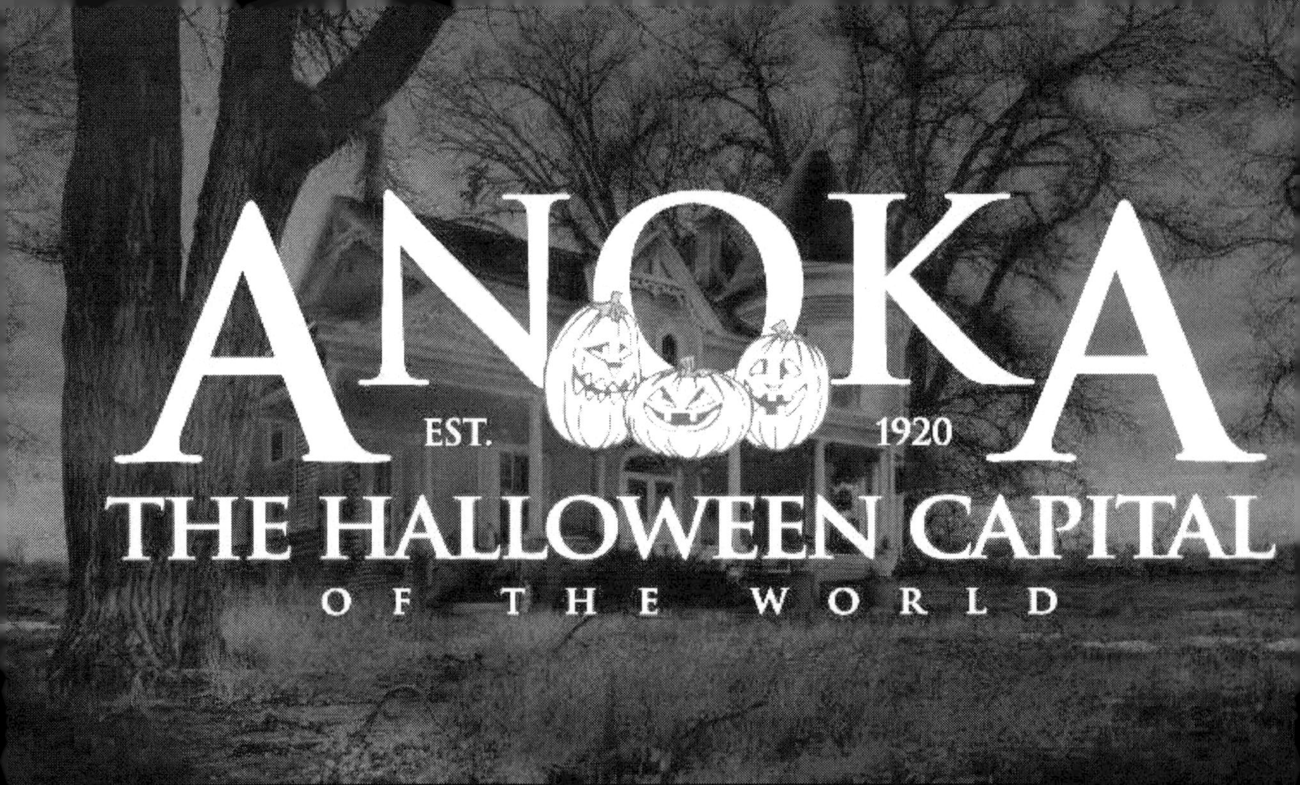
ANOKA
EST. 1920
THE HALLOWEEN CAPITAL
OF THE WORLD

The Offbeat Track

Anoka, MN - Halloween Capital of the World

By Kevin Lee Nelson

Looking for somewhere fun to celebrate Halloween this year? Can't make it to the annual Halloween festivities in Salem, Massachusetts, this year? Well, a possible substitute could be Anoka, Minnesota, the official "Halloween Capital of the World." You're probably asking yourself, *How did a small town in Minnesota become the Halloween Capital of the World?* I asked myself the same question. See, I used to live in Salem. I can tell you from experience their annual Halloween festival is HUGE. It's like a Halloween version of Mardi Gras. In fact, it's almost become too big for the city to handle. So when I found out that the sleepy little town of Anoka, MN, was the Halloween Capital, I wondered, *Really? Why not Salem?* Two reasons: first, Salem is already the "Witch Capital." Secondly, Anoka beat them to it. Their Halloween Festival is over 103 years old.

But why Anoka? Most of you have probably never heard of the town before. Well, let me tell you. Years before trick-or-treating was popularized in America most kids and young people used Halloween night as an excuse to cause mischief, a tradition going back hundreds of years to Ireland and Scotland. Immigrants brought the tradition to America and people would pull pranks, cause vandalism, and conduct all manner of delinquent behavior. It was a night of practical jokes and shenanigans. But not all Americans were as keen on the wild behavior as they were back in the old country. The pranks became so irksome in some communities, including Anoka, that officials threatened to ban the holiday.

One Halloween night about a century ago some children in Anoka thought it would be funny to set loose cows into the town's Main Street where they roamed the downtown area creating a mess. One even ended up in the county jail. The kids really took pranks to the next level and turned it into full-blown mayhem. They vandalized properties, tipped over outhouses, and managed to put a car on the Anoka County High School rooftop. This went on for years. Every November 1, Anokans would wake up to destruction and chaos. Finally, by 1920 they'd had enough.

They considered banning the holiday but figured the young ruffians would just ignore it and continue their harassment anyway. Then George Green, a local businessman, came up with the idea: what if the town hosted Halloween festivities that would divert (and hopefully replace) the annual lawlessness? They figured they'd give it a shot and planned an evening of Halloween games and fun. Some of those activities, like the "chicken catch" where live chickens were released into crowds of kids to be caught, seems rather provincial by today's standards, but it worked. Those who caught the chickens didn't get candy or prizes — they got to keep the chickens. Probably wouldn't be as popular today.

Businesses decorated their storefronts to enter a Halloween decorating contest, turning Anoka's Main St. into a giant spooky Halloween attraction. Winners of the contest didn't win caramel apples or cash. They got… *gasoline?* I suppose that would still work today. Gas cards are frequently given out as prizes these days. The town hosted a big Halloween parade and encouraged people to dress up in costume. The *Anoka County Union* documented 500 costumed Anokans crowding the streets. Children were far too busy with the grand spectacle to cause mischief and mayhem. The next day all that the people of Anoka had to clean up was confetti and streamers. It was such a wild success that they decided to do it the following year.

Anoka resident Henry Veidt told the *Anoka Herald* in 1921, "We've tried a community Halloween tonight for the second time … Last year it was a success. This year, it is even greater. I don't think there's a possible doubt but that Anoka will celebrate next Halloween the same way—only more so." Each year the festival got bigger and bigger. They've held it every year since, with the exception of the war years of 1942 and 1943.

Anoka's "Halloween Capital of the World" designation came about in 1937 when 12-year-old Harold Blair went to Washington, DC, seeking official recognition for Anoka. In 2002 Minnesota congressman Bill Luther asked Congress to reaffirm the proclamation that Anoka is the "Halloween Capital of the World," in the House of Representatives so there would be no doubt. Luther told members of Congress, "Anoka is thought to be the first to put on a citywide celebration and parade to provide families with alternative activities and fun on Halloween … Due to the celebration's size and community significance, Anoka first proclaimed itself the 'Halloween Capital of the World' in 1937."

While there were certainly other Halloween celebrations long before Minnesota was even a state, Anoka is the largest and longest-running Halloween celebration in the nation with a month-long schedule of events throughout October, though I think Salem might be catching up and could give them a run for their money. Even so, Anoka gets to keep the title. Besides, what's wrong with two massive Halloween celebrations? I'm certainly not complaining.

Resources and Works Consulted:

City of Anoka. https://anokahalloween.com/history/.

Raemont, Nina. *"How Anoka Became the Halloween Capital of the World"*. Mpls St. Paul Magazine. https://mspmag.com/arts-and-culture/how-anoka-became-the-halloween-capital-of-the-world/.

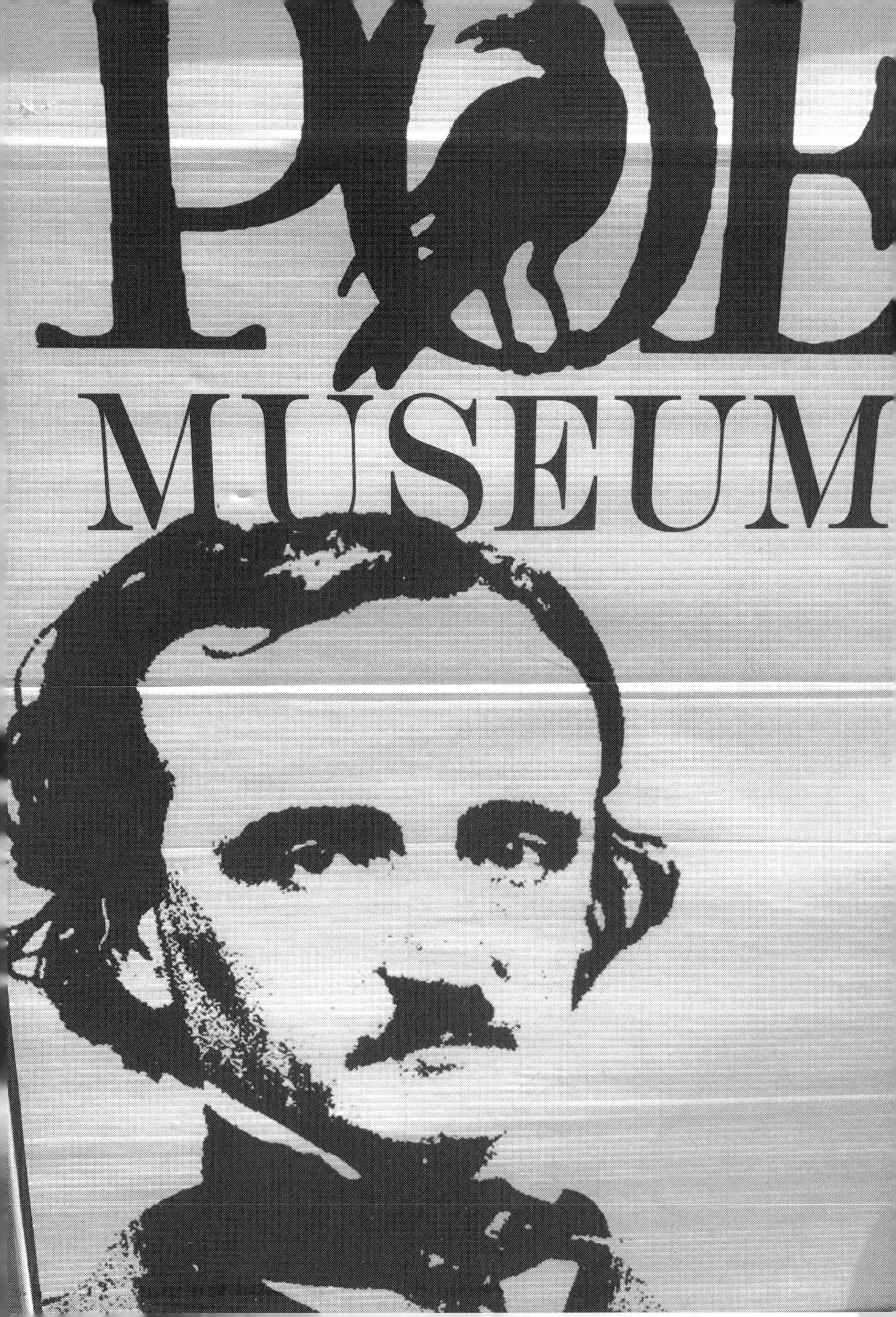
POE
MUSEUM

Behind This Curtain

The Poe Museum, Richmond, Virginia

By David Weatherly

Located in the Shockoe Bottom neighborhood of Richmond, Virginia, the Poe Museum pays tribute to the great American writer Edgar Allan Poe. The museum holds one of the world's largest collections of documents related to Poe, including letters, original manuscripts, and first editions of his works. In addition, the museum has many of Poe's personal belongings as well as various memorabilia related to his life and work.

The beginnings of the museum date back to 1906 when the Poe Memorial Association tried, and failed, to generate public interest in building a monument for the writer. Poe was considered a disreputable character and at the time, city officials had no desire or motivation to pay him any tribute.

Ten years later, the group re-formed to save the building that had housed the *Southern Literary Messenger*. The publication was notable for Poe historians because it was the place where the writer's career in journalism had started. The city had plans to tear down the messenger building and, despite the Memorial Association's work, officials went ahead with their plan and demolished the structure. James Howard Whitty, the group's organizer, managed to salvage material from the building. He hoped to use the material later at another location for something Poe related. As it turned out, the material was utilized. Historic preservationists Archer and Annie Jones helped arrange the building of a Poe memorial garden with the materials that Whitty had salvaged. The garden was erected in a vacant lot behind a landmark known as the Old Stone House.

The Poe Shrine opened on the grounds on April 26, 1922. Notable visitors to the shrine in its early years included Henry Miller, Salvador Dali, and weird-fiction writer H.P. Lovecraft.

The museum eventually expanded into three adjoining structures including the Elizabeth Poe Memorial Building that utilized a staircase from one of Poe's childhood homes.

Although Poe never lived in the building, the site seemed to be a fitting one with a lot of history of its own. Constructed around 1740, the Old Stone House is noted as being the oldest residential building in the city. The house was built by a German immigrant named Jacob Ege. Ege built the home for his bride, Maria Dorethea Scheerer. Records indicate that there were additions to the structure in 1754. According to tax records from 1782, the home was still in the Ege family and was by that time owned by Jacob's son, Samuel.

In 1824, the Marquis de Lafayette paid a visit to Richmond. Accompanying him was a volunteer company of young Richmond men known as the Junior Morgan Riflemen. One of the riflemen was a fifteen-year-old named Edgar Allan Poe. The riflemen stood as part of Lafayette's honor guard outside of the Ege house while the Marquis visited with the family.

It's unlikely that Poe entered the home during this time, and it's unknown whether or not he ever visited the Ege family in later years, but he was at least around the house and the sites of his own Richmond homes are nearby. Also close by is the grave of Poe's mother, Eliza, who is buried in the graveyard of St. John's Church in Richmond's Church Hill neighborhood.

The Old Stone House has some mysteries of its own. One is a curious insignia to the right of the east window on the home's south side. The insignia, "IR," has caused a lot of speculation and theories over the years. Some believe that it stands for "Jacobus Rex," which means "King James." This would imply the house was built during the reign of King James II (1658-1688).

Others suggest that the stone was left by English privateer Christopher Newport when he brought settlers for the Virginia Company to the region in 1607. A more likely theory is that the stone was found washed ashore from one of the many ships coming into the area's ports.

It should come as no surprise that a place associated with Edgar Allan Poe is haunted. For decades now, there have been stories of ghosts at the museum.

The museum claims to have the largest collection of Poe related items in the world and it certainly has some unusual pieces including articles of his clothing and a lock of his hair collected after his death, and it's believed that some of these items themselves could be haunted. One item of note is one of Poe's walking sticks. The stick is often pointed to as the focus of a shadow figure that's been seen in the hallways, in the garden and on the grounds, a figure that many people believe is the spirit of Edgar Allan Poe himself.

Some visitors have reported catching the shadow man in the background of photographs taken around the museum.

Another potentially haunted item is a hand mirror that belonged to Poe's wife Virginia, though no one has claimed that her spirit is present; rather, they think it may be Mr. Poe who stays close to the item, longing, perhaps, for his wife.

One story of ghosts at the site involves an incident with a shipment of Edgar Allan Poe bobblehead figures. The shipment had not been unpacked the day it arrived but was left for the following day. Employees who came in to open the museum the next morning found that the bobbleheads had been unpacked and lined up on the shelves for display. None of the employees had unpacked the shipment, and no one had been in the museum since it had shut the previous evening. The burglar alarm was never tripped that night so some assume that the spirit of Poe must have unpacked the little figures of himself.

The entry for the museum on the Hauntedplaces.org website has a comment from a user named Rachel who says that she is a former employee of the museum. Rachel writes:

"One afternoon, I was working in the gift shop and Mr. Poe's face appeared in water stains on the wall and then disappeared."

Rachel also reports that on a separate occasion, she felt heavy breathing on her neck although no living creature was present. Just after this incident, she heard a "horrible scream" that rang in her ears.

A pair of ghost children have also been reported around the museum. They're both blonde and thought to be the children of the home's original owners. They too have reportedly shown up in visitor photographs.

The museum is a must see for anyone with an interest in weird fiction, American history, literature, and of course, Edgar Allan Poe and his legacy. If you visit, you may well see one or both of the museum's black cats—Edgar and Pluto. They were found by the facility's gardener when they were kittens and adopted by the staff. They have free reign of the grounds and are well cared for, a fitting tribute in many ways since Poe himself loved cats.

As a curiosity itself, the museum is a fitting tribute to a man who led an unusual life and left behind an influential body of work. The museum continues to attract researchers, historians and enthusiasts from around the world who come to see the collection. The museum also hosts regular events including "Unhappy Hour" gatherings in the garden. A schedule and more information is available on their website listed below.

The Poe Museum is located at:

1914 E. Main Street

Richmond, VA 23223

Resources and Works Consulted:

Hauntedplaces.org

Poemuseum.org

Silent Sentinels: Scarecrow Lore and Traditions

By Kevin Lee Nelson

When I was about six years old I watched a made-for-television horror film called *Dark Night of the Scarecrow* directed by Frank De Felitta (1981). In the film a scarecrow comes to life after being possessed by a person who was wrongfully accused of a crime and murdered by a vigilante mob. One-by-one, the scarecrow exacts revenge on those who murdered him. In the film the audience never actually sees the scarecrow do any killing — it's cleverly suggested. In fact, we never even see the scarecrow move, that is, until the final chilling shot. That scene has lived with me for over forty years and has led to a lifetime fascination with scarecrows and scarecrow lore. In grade school I would draw scarecrows in the margins of my notebooks keeping watch over my notations and homework. In college I won the university's costume contest with — you guessed it — a scarecrow costume.

From the *Wizard of Oz*, to the infamous Batman villain, *The Scarecrow*, and scores of horror films, scarecrows and harvest figures have become iconic symbols of strange rural practices and the personifications of our autumnal fears. A scarecrow's caricature of the human form places it within the so-called "uncanny valley," that is, the eerie sensation one feels when encountering a human-like simulacrum, like a manikin, ventriloquist dummy, or human-like robot — shoddy copies of ourselves, especially when a scarecrow is given the semblance of life while blown about by a night wind under an autumn moon, arms flailing and legs kicking as if it's dancing some unholy jig. That, my friends, is the stuff of nightmares.

The Origins of Scarecrows

Historians tell us the earliest scarecrows were used in Egypt over 3,000 years ago. The Egyptians constructed wooden frames covered in nets to catch birds and prevent them from destroying their crops growing along the Nile. Farmers would wear long white scarves, wave their arms, shout, and chase quail into the nets where their feet would become entangled.

The first human-looking scarecrows are believed to have appeared 500 years later in ancient Greece. The Greeks believed that a minor rustic fertility god named Priapus protected livestock and crops. The most common version of the Greek myth is that Priapus was the son of Aphrodite by Dionysus. According to legend, Hera cursed him with extreme ugliness while he was still in Aphrodite's womb. Because of his ugliness, Priapus joined Pan and the satyrs of the wood as a spirit of fertility and growth. Greek farmers erected statues of him in their fields and orchards because they believed he bestowed fertility and bounty to the land, but also because his extreme ugliness would scare away unwanted and harmful birds. The practice was copied by the Romans and eventually the tradition spread throughout Europe and hybridized with local customs.

In Europe there is strong evidence that early scarecrows were once used as sacrifices to nature spirits. During pagan times people may have been strung up in fields and sacrificed to various fertility gods, not unlike Stephen King's horror tale (and subsequent film) *The Children of the Corn*. As areas grew more Christian, particularly throughout Normandy and Brittany, life-sized effigies of Christ on the cross were set among the fields as a sacrificial proxy and served as a ward against evil spirits. The similarities between scarecrows lashed to a cross and the Crucifixion are striking. It is speculated that this was the Church's way of turning pagan populations away from barbaric customs of human sacrifices and instead provided an acceptable bloodless alternative.

In 14th century Britain young boys and the elderly were employed as living scarecrows to chase away birds during the planting season so that the birds wouldn't eat the newly planted seeds. They carried clappers and other noisemakers to scare away birds. However, by the mid 1300's the Plague had killed so many people that there were not enough young boys or elderly to perform these duties, so human-like effigies were placed in the fields instead. However, they were not nearly as effective, as clever birds quickly lost their fear of them. Scarecrows became even more common after the Industrial Revolution when many young boys, who would traditionally work as living scarecrows, were sent to work in factories and mines instead.

Scarecrows became a common part of the British rural landscape. English writer Walter Thornbury (1828-1876) wrote, "To my mind the scarecrow is a feature of the landscape that is a pleasure to look upon. Even the most humble, those that are no more than a bundle of sticks and a few rags, are a symbol of the passing seasons and, made in man's image, stand in our stead as silent observers of the glory of nature at work."

Depending on the region, scarecrows went by many different names throughout Britain. "Hodmadod" was a name for a scarecrow used mostly in Berkshire and the Isle of Wight. In Scotland the common term was "tattie-bogle". Other British scarecrow names include: "mummet," "shoy-hoy," and "mawkin." The latter term, "mawkin," refers to a bundle of rags fastened to a pole which bakers used to clean out their brick ovens before putting in the bread. It is theorized that the association with scarecrows comes from bakers that took their worn-out mawkins and stuck them in the ground where their grain was growing. The mawkins looked like stick people, and when the wind picked up, the rags would flutter in the air and scare away birds.

The second most common term for scarecrow in Britain was "jackolent," first appearing in Shakespeare's *The Merry Wives of Winsor* (1597). The name jackolent is based on a living scarecrow named Jack o'Kent who was said to have sold his soul to the devil in return for dark supernatural powers during the

Middle Ages. After his diabolical pact, Jack o'Kent became a so-called "cunning man," or warlock, with mastery over nature, the elements, and evil spirits. In the article "Wizardry on the Welsh Border" in *Folklore Magazine,* author B.A. Wherry wrote:

"Once Jack was engaged by a farmer to scare crows, but there was a fair going on in the town and Jack didn't mean to miss it, so he called all the crows together from all the fields around, and when they were all collected, he sent them into an old barn, with no roof to it. But Jack put the crows in there and said something to them, and they couldn't get out, try as they might.

So Jack, he went to the fair, but when he had been enjoying himself there a bit, he met his master. So the farmer said, 'Hullo Jack, what art thee doin' here? Didn't I tell thee to look after th' crows?' But Jack says, 'T' crows be alright, master.' And he took his master to the old barn, and sure enough there was the crows, and they couldn't get out, although that barn had no roof, until Jack told them to."

Later, a jackolent became sort of a puppet-like figure to be ridiculed and pilloried. The jackolent, which represented Winter and Death, was created in the spring around Lent and would be paraded around. People would hurl sticks at it and beat it to symbolically mock death. Eventually it was ritually destroyed to represent the end of winter and the rebirth of spring. Prior to this a live chicken was used as the object of attack and killed as a sacrificial offering to the land.

Scarecrow traditions naturally vary across the European continent, including many other types of straw effigies, or harvest figures, made at harvest time, like the "Rye Hag," "Corn Dollies," and the "Corn Wolf." They're created and taken into one's home or barn for good luck until the following year, or tossed onto a neighboring farmer's land to taunt them for being slow to harvest their fields. The Portuguese have an old superstitious belief that the best scarecrows are made entirely from straw, especially straw from a particularly bountiful harvest. In Germany there is a belief that fatter scarecrows provide better protection for crops. It's also believed to be bad luck to destroy a scarecrow after the harvest has been brought in. Instead, it should be carefully stored away in a barn over the winter. In the following spring it is given a new set of clothes and returned to the fields as soon as the fields are newly plowed. In Austria some farmers have their land and their scarecrows blessed by a local priest at the start of each growing season to ensure bountiful crops. In Italy it is taboo to dress a scarecrow in the clothes of someone who has died, especially the clothes the person died in, or the ghost of the dead person may try to inhabit the scarecrow. Ideally the clothes should come from a young man in his prime so that some of his vitality and virility can be passed on to the scarecrow and the land.

In Japan the first scarecrows were called the *kakashi* (meaning something that smells bad). Japanese farmers would construct bamboo frameworks in their fields and hang old rags, spoiled meat, and fish bones from the bamboo. They also strung pieces of bamboo and bits of metal from the framework to make noise like wind-chimes to scare away birds. Later, they were made to look more humanoid using old clothes and straw stuffing. Japanese farmers believed that their kakashi were magical. In the spring they invited the god of agriculture (*Kuebiko*) to leave his home in the mountains and possess their scarecrows to protect their crops. Even today some areas still observe an end of the season celebration called "sending off the scarecrows" (*kakashi-age*). During this ceremony farmers move their scarecrows from their fields and place them in their own yards. They place new hats on the scarecrows and give offerings of rice cakes as a "thank you" before the mountain god departs the scarecrow and returns to the mountains for the winter.

Scarecrows in the New World

Native American tribes had their own forms of scarecrows long before European colonists arrived. 19th century painter Seth Eastman captured a scene from the Dakota tribe in his watercolor painting *Guarding the Fields* (1849-1855). In the painting Dakota women act as living scarecrows from elevated and sheltered platforms inside a cornfield using rattles or noise-makers to scare away birds.

Guarding the Fields *by Seth Eastman.*

In Central America the descendants of the Aztecs have an ancient tradition of placing roughly-carved wooden hawks with outspread wings and glass eyes atop posts to frighten away birds. We see the modern equivalent of this today with the life-like plastic owls used to frighten away pesky birds from gardens and other places where birds are a nuisance. Tribes of the southwest are known to make articulated scarecrows that move with the desert winds and watch over their patches of corn and vegetables.

During colonial times many scarecrow traditions were transplanted to the New World by English colonists, mostly reflecting the same customs practiced in Britain. Thomas Jefferson mentioned his own three scarecrows guarding his corn fields in his 1826 farm guide, *The Farmbook*. Nathaniel Hawthorne wrote a fanciful story about a scarecrow brought to life in his 1852 tale “Feathertop.”

Birds were a constant problem for colonial farmers. Wise farmers would plant four kernels, as the saying goes, “one for the birds, one for the worms, and two to grow.” By the 1750s birds became such a problem that local authorities began placing bounties on crows and blackbirds. A boy could earn a shilling for each dead crow (about $10 today). By the mid-1800s so many crows and blackbirds had been shot and killed that a new problem began to arise; corn borers, worms, and other insects, which the birds had previously eaten, were now decimating crops and destroying far more corn and wheat than the birds had. Scientists urged farmers to stop killing birds, and many went back to the time-honored tradition of building scarecrows.

Fair Exchange, No Robbery *by William Sidney Mount 1865*

The Pennsylvania Germans of Eastern Pennsylvania brought over their own unique scarecrow traditions during the 19th century. They refer to their scarecrows in Pennsylvania German dialect as *Lumbemann* or *Butzemann* (or the female equivalent, *Butzefrau* and collectively as *Butzemenner*). Interestingly, there is anecdotal evidence that the term "Bogeyman" stems from the Pennsylvania German butzemann. One Pennsylvania German folktale tells about a farmer who put up a butzemann out in his field. The next day he discovered tears on the face of the butzemann. Feeling sorry for him and assuming he felt lonely, the farmer made a butzefrau wearing a bonnet and a dress and placed it next to him in the field. Even today they are often seen in pairs.

The lumbemann is a simple scarecrow, but the Butzemann is something special; it's a scarecrow in which dormant plant spirits are awakened. Some people in southeastern Pennsylvania still practice an old form of rural folk magic called pow-wow, or *braucherei*, meaning "to try." It's a distinctly American folk magic tradition drawing upon early European magical traditions, old folk remedies, and indigenous herbalism. Some practitioners, called pow-wow doctors or *brauchers*, have an annual tradition called *Butzemannsege* (honoring of the plant spirits within the scarecrow) and *Kannsege* (ceremony of the corn) which is when the plant spirits are awakened inside the scarecrow. The Kannsege is one of the most interesting scarecrow traditions I have encountered in my research.

During the Kannsege ceremony the Butzeman is given "life" through a ritual where plant spirits are invoked and invited into the scarecrow. Butzemenner are traditionally constructed on Groundhog Day from the remnants of last year's crops, often still containing seeds. A symbol is drawn with the thumb on the forehead of the Butzeman that looks similar to an Ansuz rune (ᚨ), meaning life force or breath. The braucher then breathes into the mouth of the scarecrow and they become a conduit for the plant spirits to inhabit the scarecrow. This awakens the scarecrow, essentially bringing the scarecrow to life. It is then walked around the perimeter of the property so that it learns what area it needs to protect.

As a side note, it's interesting how similar this is to the Jewish mystical tradition of creating a golem; that is, an anthropomorphic effigy, often made of clay, that is magically brought to life. In Jewish folklore a golem is created when the word *emet* (אמת), meaning "truth" is drawn on the golem's forehead bringing the effigy to life. The golem is deactivated when the first letter aleph (א) – Hebrew is read from right to left – of the word *emet* is erased, becoming *met* (מת) "dead." Golems are typically used to perform menial duties for the creator, as in the legend of the Golem of Prague, where 16th century mystic, Rabbi Loew, created a Frankenstein-like monster that eventually became uncontrollable.

Once activated, the Butzemann must be given a name. Often the name is given by the landowner, and in some cases the Butzemann names itself though various means of spirit communication. After a name has been chosen it starts a lineage of Butzemanner. For example, if the name is Johan, next year's Butzemann will be named *Johansen,* (son of Johan). In this way a lineage of scarecrows is passed from year to year, and the spiritual connection to the original one created on that acreage of land makes it easier for the plant spirits to take possession of the new Butzemann at the beginning of each growing season, like sliding into a familiar skin.

Next, oaths are given to the Butzemann outlining how it will be honored throughout the growing season with gifts of cream, honey, mead, flowers, and clothes. Among the oaths, the single most important oath is the promise that the Butzemann will be released from its duties by being ritually burned no later than October 30th. Any offerings given to the scarecrow must also be burned. There are legends of hobos and tramps stealing clothes from a Butzemann and being hexed or haunted by the scarecrow. Another legend tells of a woman who intentionally stole some fabric from a Butzemann, made some patches from it, and sewed the patches into a quilt. Then she gave the quilt to a person she disliked. It was essentially a hex, or a curse, on the person who received the spiritually tainted quilt.

Typically the Butzemann is ritually burned between the Autumnal Equinox and Oct 30. However, if one fails to do this, and the Butzemann is allowed to remain intact until Halloween, it is believed the beneficial plant spirits will depart, leaving an empty shell for evil spirits to inhabit on Halloween night, resulting in the scarecrows becoming uncontrollable and very dangerous. Pennsylvania German country is full of legends about Butzemanner that were not destroyed by Halloween. Even today it is common in many households to scare children to behave by saying, "The Butzemann (Bogeyman) will get you!"

Contemporary Harvest Figures

Today scarecrows are very uncommon on farms in America unless they are guarding a small garden patch or serving as a seasonal decoration. There is little use for scarecrows now that most industrial farms use seeds treated with Avipel, an organic compound that causes birds to experience temporary digestive distress after eating them. Birds quickly learn to avoid eating the seeds. Without the risk of birds ruining crops who needs a scarecrow? Yet the tradition of building scarecrows carries on in the form of harvest figures. Contemporary scarecrows typically aren't practical agricultural constructs; they're a celebrated form of folk-art, at least in the autumn. Instead of doing a job in rural fields, today scarecrows take up residence in front yards. One can find them propped up near a patch of pumpkins, tied to lamp posts, or slouched in a porch chair. The once utilitarian scarecrow is now mostly a symbolic harvest figure that personifies the autumn season and the bounty of the fall harvest.

The crafting of harvest figures is primarily a feature of rural areas and small towns that still have connections to country life. Their annual construction is perhaps an unconscious homage to forgotten harvest gods and dimly remembered Old World traditions. In the past, late summer and early autumn was a time when food was plentiful. People could afford to relax and enjoy the fruits of their labor. It was a time for jubilation: parties, games, and a bit of tomfoolery. Now, the crafting of harvest figures is a popular creative outlet for amusement and whimsical expression, but it also taps into old folk practices, connecting people to the season, the land, and tradition. Harvest figures also embody a bit of the strange and sinister, which is naturally where minds turn as the days grow shorter and Halloween approaches. They remind us of our mortality, as they are a caricature of a human lifespan compressed into a single season: birth, a time in the sun, and eventual decay.

In recent years "Scarecrow Festivals" have become a popular event in communities across the nation. Scarecrow aficionados can find annual scarecrow festivals in: Phelps, WI, St. Charles, IL, Brenham, TX, Stevensville, MT, Coburg, OR, Coshoctan, OH, Lahaska, PA, and especially in Hoschton, GA, known as the Scarecrow Capital of the World. Parades, hayrides, games, costuming, and scarecrow-building contests are common features at these festivals. In some communities entire downtowns are taken over by scarecrows, creating an odd tableau where the normal townsfolk appear replaced by eerie, still, and straw-stuffed imitations.

Harvest figures do not last long after Thanksgiving. Nor are they meant to. They are ephemeral effigies constructed of remnants, harvest produce, and maybe a little magic. Their pumpkin heads begin to blacken and rot; their faded clothes get soggy and mildewed; their innards of straw and leaves slowly molder. Eventually they return to the land. The harvest figure has served its purpose. Then, as the season passes into winter, a new seasonal effigy will take its place, *the snowman.*

Resources and Works Consulted:

Dark Night of the Scarecrow. Directed by Frank De Felitta. Wizan Productions. 1981.

Giblin, James, & Ferguson, Dale. *The Scarecrow Book*.

Haining, Peter. *The Scarecrow: Fact and Fable*. 1988.

Jefferson, Thomas. *The Farm Book*. 1826.

Neal, Avon, & Parker, Ann. *Ephemeral Folk Figures: Scarecrows, Harvest Figures, and Snowmen*. 1969.

Rushing, Felder. *Scarecrows: Making Harvest Figures and Other Yard Folks*. 1998.

Schreiwer, Robert. "Entschtanning 8: Butzemann, Butzemannsege, Kannsege." Urglaawe. https://urglaawe.blogspot.com/2020/02/entschtanning-8-butzemann-butzemannsege.html.

Virag, Irene. "We're off to see the Mawkin." *Newsday*. October, 17 1996.

Wherry, B.A. "Wizardry on the Welsh Border." *Folklore Magazine*, # 32. 1932.

A Trick in Your Treat: Exploring the History of Tainted Halloween Candy

By Chad Lewis

It was the 1980s, and after weeks of anticipation, Halloween night finally arrived for millions of excited kids throughout the country. A palpable fear permeated through the hordes of little witches, werewolves, and superheroes, as fate seemed hell-bent on ruining their entire night. You see, this last stop on their trick-or-treat route was not meant to add to their plunder of sugary treats. Instead, this all important waylay was aimed at calming the frazzled nerves of their terrified parents. As the hospital staff painstakingly sent each kid's collection of goodies through the X-ray machines, parents braced for the worst. Believe it or not, parents in the 1980s clamored to spend the last hours of Halloween at the local hospital. By no means was this fear isolated to a certain city or state, or even an entire region. Throughout the 1980s, newspapers around the country published articles detailing the locations where parents could get their kids' candy checked out by medical professionals. On October 31, 1985, the *St Louis Post-Dispatch* ran an article titled "Warnings to Young Goblins," in which the paper told of several local hospitals that were offering free x-rays of Halloween candy.

For a kid, nothing can kill the excitement and danger of Halloween night as quickly as standing in line at the hospital instead of wolfing down your hard-earned surgary treats as you and your friends trade away your least liked candy. I know this to be a fact, because when I was young, my mother fell victim to the hysteria sweeping the country and dragged my brother and me to our local hospital to ensure that our candy was safe to eat. I have a fuzzy memory of impatiently standing in line in a sterile hospital room as a concerned nurse instructed us not to eat anything from our bag of goodies until it was deemed safe. Luckily, as an adult, I seemed to have almost completely repressed this unnecessary memory, which was only jogged when I began researching this topic. Unfortunately for my older brother, the memory of this unproductive act is still all too clear, and he was able to fill in some blank spots in my memory.

Amazingly, while most of today's children have not been exposed to the indignities of not eating your Halloween candy as soon as it leaves the candy giver's hand, getting your candy x-rayed wasn't just some 1980s flash in the pan phenomenon. I found articles touting this service from up to this very day. For their October 14, 2022, paper, the *Mount Carmel Register* informed readers who wanted to bring their candy in to be x-rayed to be prepared for a little wait "if staff are busy x-raying patients." Although the heyday of our irrational tainted Halloween candy fear is long behind us, it is certainly not extinct.

What is behind this crazed frenzy for parents to have the medical profession certify their kids' candy as being safe? For that answer we must take a deep dive into unfounded parental hysteria, fear mongering by the media, and a couple of isolated events that looked to forever change the way American children enjoyed the scariest night of the year!

For the past several decades, in the weeks leading up to Halloween, the media has been bombarding the nation with dire warnings that demented individuals were going to hand out poisoned candy in order to kill and harm as many innocent children as possible. Media outlets throughout the nation give out constant warnings that parents need to be vigilant against razor blades in apples, needles in candy bars, and poisoned homemade treats. Are these fears overhyped and unfounded? Well, let's start from the beginning.

In the 1980s, Joel Best, a professor in the department of sociology and criminal justice at the University of Delaware, began researching the issue of tainted Halloween candy, and quickly became the go to person for media outlets that were clamoring for some poisoned candy stories to horrify the general public with. The only wrench in this plan was that Professor Best was unable to find any actual accounts of kids dying due to a stranger giving them tainted Halloween candy. In fact, after 30 years of researching the topic, Best has never been able to verify even one death caused by stranger danger candy. However, that is not to say that numerous individuals haven't tried to spread death and chaos during Halloween---it just doesn't come at the hands of strangers—because Halloween mischief and death is much more sinister, because it originates from the minds of our own loved ones.

I am sure that throughout the history of trick-or-treating in America there were countless local neighborhood incidents of people handing out inedible candy. Perhaps the old widow living alone in the dark house used salt instead of sugar in her cookies, or the eccentric old man in the creepy big house on the hill gave especially bitter candies to the children. Yet, these cases would have been brushed off as the price you pay for going to houses/people you should have known to avoid.

The absence of any deaths caused by stranger danger Halloween candy does not mean that all Halloween candy is 100% safe. What it does mean is that you are far more likely to get hit by a car while trick-or-treating than you are to get some weird candy…unless of course you visit the homes of these next people.

The Demented Doctor

Leave it to a doctor to upend their Hippocratic Oath and kick off the first widely-known case of Halloween candy tampering. In 1959, Doctor William Shyne decided to play a little Halloween trick of his own. The Centerville, California, man was charged for handing out laxative-coated candies to more than 30 youngsters. The irony here is that Mr. Shyne was a dentist, and if he had just stuck to handing out surgary treats, he may have created more business for himself. Worse yet, the doctor was able to convince Mrs. Hazel Engelby, a nurse, to help with his devious plans. Of those who were on the receiving end of this sinister trickery, the Gazette reported "Some of the children vomited; others came down with diarrhea." Fortunately for the Halloween hating pair, no one was severely harmed by their ill-conceived plan. For his punishment, the *York Dispatch* reported that the good doctor was "fined $525, placed on two-years' probation, and given a four-months suspended jail sentence." The charges against Mrs. Engelby were dropped. Although neither of them served any jail time, when it comes to their legacy, both have been given a life-sentence for being known as the crazed people who tried to destroy trick-or-treating.

Trick or Treating is for the Young

In 1964, if you were unlucky enough to visit the home of Helen Pfeil on Halloween night you would not have been pleased with her candy selection. The 47-year-old housewife seemed to love all the young costumed kids that were coming to her door, as evidenced by the *Fresno Bee*, which quoted her husband as saying that his wife "loved children and had been giving the younger ones candy all day." Ok, so she loved little kids, but what about the older trick or treaters? Well, according to the *Tampa Tribune* those unfortunate souls got "giveaway packages containing ant traps, metal mesh scrubbing pads, and dog biscuits." Apparently, Mrs. Pfeil strongly believed that older kids should not participate in the ritual. Like most criminals, Mrs. Pfeil did not do a good job at covering her tracks. Even though the rat buttons she included in her bags resembled bottle caps candy, the ones she handed out plainly stated "Poison—Keep away from children and pets." Thankfully, the authorities were able to retrieve all 12 of her tainted giveaway packages before any serious physical harm was caused. Mrs. Pfeil was arrested and eventually pleaded guilty to two misdemeanor counts of endangering the life and health of a child. I was a bit surprised to discover that the disdain of older trick or treaters was not a more modern phenomenon. I wonder how Ms. Pfei would feel about the recent trend of offering parents who accompany their little trick or treaters beer, shots, and other adult beverages.

Heroin in the Candy!

In 1970, the *Miami News* newspaper ran the headline "Heroin-laced candy kills child" while telling the tragic story of 5-year-old Kevin Totson. Newspapers from around the country picked up on the frightening story of some demented lunatic giving out heroin-laced candy treats. Apparently, Kevin had gone out trick-or-treating with his two brothers. After one hour of traveling the neighborhood, the threesome came home. Kevin's mother, Ida Foster, told the newspaper, "The boys carefully sorted through their candy that was improperly wrapped or was open." Adding to the family's thoroughness was the report from the *Muscatine Journal* that Kevin "even threw out the apples because he thought there might be razor blades in them."

After eating a few pieces of his candy, Kevin fell asleep just before 11pm. A few hours later Kevin was discovered sweating and breathing heavily. No matter what the family tried, they could not awaken the young boy, so they rushed him to the hospital.

Even before the forensic testing on the candy was completed, Ms. Foster was railing against the dangers of Halloween. The *Abilene Reporter-News* ran a quote from her saying, "They've got to rule out Halloween…it's too dangerous for kids." When the test did come back, traces of both heroin and quinine were found. Unfortunately, Kevin did not survive, putting a sorrowful exclamation point on his mother's dire warning about Halloween.

This would have been the perfect cautionary tale against the dangers of Halloween if not for the November 10 article in the *Herald-Palladium* in which they reported that the death of young Kevin was not caused by Halloween candy. Instead, the young boy had "accidently swallowed a capsule while visiting his uncle's home." Looking to cover his tracks, Kevin's uncle sprinkled some additional heroin on the Halloween candy to make it look like a random occurrence. Unfortunately, the damage to Halloween had already been done, giving more ammunition for those looking to put an end to the holiday.

The Candyman Can

The most heartbreaking story on this list belongs to a Mr. Ronald Clark O'Bryan. The year was 1974, and like any loving father Mr. Clark wanted to take his eight-year-old son Timothy and his five-year-old daughter Elizabeth trick-or-treating in the Texas neighborhood near Pasadena —right outside of Houston. The happy family was joined by Jim Bates, a family friend, and his two children. The group swiftly moved from door to door grabbing as much candy as they could, and when they got no response from a darkened house, the group quickly pressed on. Everyone except Mr. O'Bryan that is---he stubbornly remained at the door, refusing to give up. A minute later he caught back up to the group and proudly showed off five large Pixy Stix tubes that were a reward for his patience at the previous house. Unfortunately, after only making it to a couple blocks of houses, rainy weather cut short their Halloween fun and the family retreated back to the Bates home where Mr. O'Bryan proudly handed out the prized Pixy Stix to the four children. The last tube of sugar was given to a neighborhood kid (that the family knew) who happened to be still out trick-or-treating.

Upon returning home, according to *The Deer Park Progress*, the O'Bryan children were allowed to enjoy one treat from their Halloween haul. Timothy shot right for the Pixy Stix and within minutes of consuming the awful tasting treat "complained of severe abdominal pain. He vomited, went into convulsions and lost consciousness." The *Cincinnati Enquirer* carried a quote from Mr. O'Bryan who tried to explain what had happened with a more personal perspective, stating "Thirty seconds after I left Tim's room, I heard him cry to me. 'Daddy, Daddy, my stomach hurts….' He was in the bathroom, convulsing, vomiting and gasping and then suddenly he went limp." By the time Timothy reached the hospital, his fate had already been sealed.

Investigators began frantically trying to collect the remaining Pixy Stix, which thankfully had not been consumed by any of the other children. Once the police were able to rule out any of the houses along the families' route, suspicion turned to Mr. O'Bryan. It was uncovered that a few months prior to going out for Halloween, he had taken out life insurance policies on his children and that he was up to his neck in debt. Lab reports found that the candy had been laced with enough cyanide to kill two full-grown humans. To make matters worse, witness after witness came forward to tell of their conversation with Mr. O'Bryan about where he could obtain cyanide. This case is filled with so many twists, turns, and fascinating details, that an entire book could be written about it., but for the sake of brevity, here is how the case concluded.

As you might have easily guessed, O'Bryan was arrested for the murder of his son and the attempted murders of the other children. On June 3, 1975, a jury convicted O'Bryan and sentenced him to death. Roughly ten years after killing his son with tainted Halloween candy, O'Bryan was executed by lethal injection.

To this very day, Ronald O'Bryan is widely referred to as the man who killed Halloween.

Final Thoughts

Although the above-mentioned cases received the most media attention and helped fuel public hysteria, they are by no means the complete list of tainted candy stories. Nearly every year, newspapers around the country are filled with Halloween stories of sewing needles discovered in candy and razor blades in apples. Even though the vast majority of these cases have turned out to be hoaxes, the legends continue to outpace the facts behind the real events. Have you ever tried to put a razor in a piece of candy or apple? It is not an easy thing to accomplish, especially so if your goal is to not damage the product in the process. Hopefully this article will help you relax and rest easy on Halloween night, knowing that the odds of a stranger providing you with poisoned candy are nearly zero.

However, like most urban legends, these fears and beliefs never completely die out. Instead, they morph and progress to keep up with the ever-changing culture in which they permeate. With the near extinction of homemade treats and unpackaged candy, something else has stepped in to fill the role of being the Halloween bogeyman---marijuana edibles and fentanyl laced candies. The show, or in this case, fear and hysteria, must go on!

Resources and Works Consulted:

Abilene Reporter-News. November 6, 1970.

Cincinnati Enquirer. November 6, 1974.

Deer Park Progress. November 7, 1974.

Fresno Bee. November 2, 1964.

Herald-Palladium. November 10, 1970.

Miami News. November 11, 1970.

Mount Carmel Register. October 14, 2022.

Muscatine Journal. November 6, 1970.

St. Louis Post-Dispatch. October 31, 1985.

Tampa Tribune. November 2, 1964.

The Gazette. November 6, 1959.

www.joelbest.net/halloween-sadism

York Dispatch. January 26, 1960.

Pumpkin Lore and the Origins of the Jack-O'-Lantern

By David Weatherly

Tis the season! Halloween season that is, and certainly the most recognizable symbol of the spooky time of the year is the smiling jack-o'-lantern.

Every year as the first hints of Autumn start to arrive, pumpkins start showing up in grocery stores and markets. They're so popular as decorative items that you can find pumpkins, and of course jack-o'-lanterns, made of resin, plastic, paper, foam and other materials, as well as finding the real thing on market shelves for those who want to carve their own masterpieces.

By the time October comes around, (for some enthusiasts late September), carved and lighted jack-o'-lanterns start turning up on front porches, in yards, and around the homes of people all across America.

Despite their popularity, many people still don't know the history of the orange Halloween symbol. Jack-o'-lanterns are a fascinating blend of Irish folklore and New World creation, and their origins might surprise you.

Halloween itself is strongly linked to the Celtic festival of Samhain, a celebration of the end of the harvest season and the beginning of the dark half of the year. Traditionally, it was thought to be a time when spirits would wander the earth, and the living had to take precautions against any malevolent forces that might come around.

Huge bonfires were built around the community as part of the celebration and to keep away any dark spirits. Somewhere along the way, the practice of keeping lanterns became part of the tradition and another symbol of protection from dark forces.

When Irish people immigrated to America, they brought the lantern tradition with them from the Emerald Isle.

Some researchers believe that the term jack-o'-lantern didn't originate in Ireland, but in England. Some evidence suggests that in 17th century Britain, a nightwatchman, who would have carried a lantern, was often called "Jack with the lantern," or "Jack of the lantern," which got shortened to "Jack-o'-lantern."

Jack was a common name in the British Isles, and it became a catchall name to use if someone's name was not known. The name Jack also shows up in a lot of traditional English folklore. Jack of the Green, Jack Frost, Jack in Irons, the list goes on—so it's certainly possible that a lantern-carrying watchman became Jack-o'-lantern. Still, the Irish would quickly dispute any such claim to the original use of the term.

An article the October 27, 1885, edition of *Harper's Young People*, gives us the following early mention of lighted pumpkins in America, giving them British roots instead of Irish:

"It is an ancient British custom to light great bonfires (Bone-fire to clear before Winter froze the ground) on Hallowe'en, and carry blazing fagots about on long poles; but in place of this, American boys delight in the funny grinning jack-o'-lanterns made of huge yellow pumpkins with a candle inside."

Pumpkins certainly weren't the first things used to make lanterns. The custom of carving vegetables and placing a candle inside as a makeshift lantern reportedly goes back centuries. An early mention of such lanterns come from a letter written in 1640 by English author James Howell. Howell mentions "a turnip cut like a Death's-head with a Candle in't." According to the writer, the lantern terrified "boys and women."

The first such lanterns were carved turnips, and if you think you've seen some creepy pumpkin jack-o'-lanterns, well, let's just say you ain't seen nothing yet!

Records indicate that in the 18th century, in Worcestershire, England, people carved faces in turnips and placed the stump of a candle inside it creating what was called Hoberdy's Lantern.

Author William Holloway mentions the use of turnips as lanterns in his 1839 *General Dictionary of Provincialisms*. He writes:

"Jack-in-the-Lanthorn, *s.* In Hampshire, boys, of a dark night, get a large turnip and scooping out the inside, make two holes in it to resemble eyes and one for a mouth, when they place a lighted candle within side, and put it on a wall or post so that it may appear like the head of a man. The chief end (and that a very bad one) is to take some younger boy than the rest, and who is not in on the secret, to show it to him with a view to frighten him."

Other vegetables used included potatoes, beets and rutabagas, but once the Irish came to America, they discovered something much bigger and better to use—the pumpkin.

The British claims to the origin of the jack-o'-lantern don't hold a candle to the full-blown folktale that came from Ireland, a tale connected to both the mysterious lanterns used every Halloween and to the devil himself.

The Tale of Stingy Jack

Stingy Jack was a nasty man. A blacksmith by trade and a drunkard by habit, Jack was always looking for a way to take advantage of people and situations and in this singular thing, he was a success.

One day, Jack was drinking in the local pub when a mysterious man in dark clothing walked in. The man sat down with Jack, and the blacksmith soon learned that he was sitting with the devil—who had come to collect Jack's soul.

If anything, Jack was a shrewd fellow and he convinced old Nick to let him have one last drink before they went off to the fiery depths. The devil agreed and joined Jack for a drink—or several. When the bill arrived, Jack suggested that they pull a trick to avoid paying the tab. Since the devil could turn into anything he wanted to, Jack told him to turn into a coin that could be used to pay for the drinks. Afterwards, the devil could turn back into himself, and the barkeep's coin would be gone. Of course, the devil liked the idea of ripping someone off, so he agreed to the stunt and turned himself into a silver coin. Instead of handing the coin over to the pub owner, Jack put the coin in his pocket next to a cross. The devil was trapped. Unable to change back, the devil pleaded with Jack to set him free. The man agreed under the condition that the devil would leave him alone for ten years. The devil reluctantly agreed, and Jack set him free. Some said that the devil liked Jack because of his cleverness and lack of scruples.

Ten years passed and Jack's number came up again. Once more, the devil came calling to collect his soul. This time, he came across Jack in a field and told the man it was time to go. "It's going to be a long trip down there," Jack commented, asking for something to eat before they left. The man pointed to an apple tree and suggested that the devil could easily climb up to the top and get an apple before they left. The devil apparently hadn't learned much from his previous dealing with Jack, and he agreed to climb the tree. As soon as he was up in the branches, Jack quickly carved crosses on the trunk of the tree, making it impossible for the devil to come back down. Trapped once again, the devil had no choice but to once more make a deal with the blacksmith. This time, Jack made the devil agree to never collect his soul, guaranteeing that he would never have to go to hell. The devil agreed and was set free.

One would think this was the end of Jack and the devil's dealings, but it wasn't. The man may have outsmarted the Prince of Hell, but he couldn't pull any tricks when he finally died and found himself upstairs at the pearly gates. It turned out that Jack was considered too sinful to be allowed into heaven. He was cast away and sent to hell as one would expect. However, while others found a warm reception in hell, Jack did not. The devil held to his word and refused to let Jack enter his domain. Barred from entry to both heaven and hell, Jack was now stuck with nowhere to go, and his spirit was sent to wander the earth, never finding any rest. As a final taunt, the devil threw Jack a hellish coal to light his way, a piece of coal that would burn forever just as the man was doomed to wander eternally.

Stingy Jack scooped out the insides of a turnip and placed the hellish coal inside, creating a makeshift lantern to carry with him as he roamed the world of the living.

Some modern researchers argue that the story of Stingy Jack who is also known as "Drunk Jack," "Jack the Smith," and other variations, is a later tale with a Christian basis that shouldn't be connected to the earlier Celtic pagan beliefs while others claim that it could be a retelling of a much earlier tale.

There's no doubt the story is an old one, originally passed down through oral tradition. A report from the Belfast Naturalists Field Club published in 1894 lists Stingy Jack as one of the potential identities of bog lights, reporting:

"He is the spirit of a man who was very wicked on earth, and also managed to trick and outwit the devil; and, in fact, made himself so feared by the Prince of Darkness, that after death he could not enter heaven, nor was even allowed into the other place, so afraid of him were the authorities there, and he must, therefore, wander about with his torch over dreary bogs and wastes forever."

As for the aforementioned bog lights, they too are a part of the overall jack-o'-lantern mythos. Known by a wide range of names from will-o-the-wisps, fox fire, fairy fire and bog lights, to corpse candles, hobby lanterns and hinkypunks, the lights appear as a glowing orb that seems to bounce around in the air creating an eerie effect.

The phosphorescent lights manifest over peat bogs, marshes and swampy ground hovering above the surface at night. Scientists use the Latin term ignis fatuus for the lights and say they're nothing mysterious, but simply a swamp gas produced by decomposing organic matter that creates combustible gases. Experts say the lights move away from people who pursue them because the gases are pushed forward by a person's breath.

In older times, the lights were thought to be the spirits of condemned souls wandering about on the earth plane and trying to lure other people away to their deaths. Those who called the lights corpse candles believed the lights were an omen of coming death.

The lights were malicious fairies, according to an article in the Belfast

Naturalists Field Club's annual report for 1894:

"Will o' the Wisp, or Jack o' Lantern as he is called in some places, and in parts of Ireland the Water Sherrie, is a kind of malicious fairy, who, by showing a light in marshes and dangerous bogs, lures benighted travelers into danger, and sometimes to death."

Somewhere along the way, the tale of Stingy Jack became connected to the mysterious lights on the bogs. This was likely due to the lantern that Jack carried about. Surely, locals thought, the odd glowing orb was old Jack wandering around in the night hoping to lead mortal souls astray. It was believed that because of his miserable existence, Jack reveled in luring people out onto the bogs and marshes late at night, staying just ahead of the person in order to pull them farther and farther off path. This could, of course, prove deadly since the person could fall into the water or into a sinkhole and be lost in darkness.

When the carving of lanterns became popular and melded with the trickery of Halloween, some kids would wander off the roads and hide out of sight while waving their lanterns about in the darkness hoping to scare younger children into believing that Stingy Jack was roaming about looking for victims.

Jack-O'-Lanterns Everywhere

Jack-o'-lanterns were once said to have certain magical powers and were used to ward off evil spirits. It was thought that they would keep away ghosts, the undead and even vampires. Purportedly, the light from a jack-o'-lantern could identify a vampire, giving humans a glimpse at the thing's true nature and causing the bloodsuckers to abandon their hunt. Whether you believe in this or not, there's no doubt that there's something magical about jack-o'-lanterns and at the least, they've had staying power. They dominate the Halloween season now, but looking back through history, we can see their development as an important symbol of the season.

Of curious note is the fact that many adaptations of Washington Irving's classic short story, *The Legend of Sleepy Hollow*, (1820) often depict the headless horseman with a jack-o'-lantern in place of his severed head.

There was no jack-o'-lantern in the original tale and Irving doesn't even mention Halloween in the story. There is a shattered pumpkin found next to Ichabod Crane's lost hat on the morning after his dreadful encounter with the horseman.

The jack-o'-lantern is, however, mentioned in Nathaniel Hawthorne's 1835 short story *The Great Carbuncle*. Hawthorne writes:

"Hide it under they cloak, say'st thou? Why, it will gleam through the holes, and make thee look like a jack-o'-lantern."

Some researchers think that Hawthorne may have been referring to the lights seen on the marshes and not the carved pumpkin version of the jack-o'-lantern, but either way, it serves as an early use of the term.

The first American depiction of what we know as a jack-o'-lantern appeared in the November 23, 1867, issue of *Harper's Weekly*. The accompanying article, titled "A Pumpkin Effigy," didn't call the carved gourd by its now common name, nor did it reference Halloween.

According to an article in the *Irish Times*, the first definitive reference to the pumpkin version of the jack-o'-lantern in conjunction with Halloween appeared in 1886 in the *Daily News*, a Canadian paper out of Kingston, Ontario, which reported:

"The old time custom of keeping up Hallowe'en was not forgotten last night by youngsters of the city. They had their maskings and their merry-makings, and perambulated the streets after dark in a way which was no doubt amusing to themselves. There was a great sacrifice of pumpkins from which to make transparent heads and face, lighted up by the unfailing two inches of tallow candle" (November 1, 1886).

In 1892, jack-o'-lanterns showed up at a high-profile celebration hosted by the mayor of Atlanta, Georgia. As part of the decorations the mayor's wife arranged, she had a number of pumpkins, carved with faces and lit from within by candles, placed around the party.

An 1895 article about Thanksgiving in the *New York Times* (November 24, 1895) suggested that lit jack-o'-lanterns should be handed out as prizes for children in Thanksgiving games.

In 1966, the television Halloween special "It's the Great Pumpkin, Charlie Brown" aired. The special introduced the idea of a Great Pumpkin that, according to the Peanuts character Linus, "rises out of the pumpkin patch and flies through the air and brings toys to all the children in the world."

The show has become a beloved holiday special and continues to air each year, for old and new generations alike. The show also further cemented the pumpkin's connection to modern Halloween celebrations.

Folklore and Curiosities

Pumpkins go hand in hand with the fall season in the United States and they're big business. Harvested in the Autumn and used for Halloween, by November, they're a big part of meals and are used in breads, soups, various des-

-serts and, of course, the classic pumpkin pies! Pumpkins are said to be one of the most versatile foods on the planet; even the yellow-orange flowers that bloom on the pumpkin vine are edible, and people all over roast pumpkin seeds as a healthy and tasty snack. Demand is high and the United States grows over 1.5 billion pounds of pumpkins each year.

The "Pumpkin Capital of the World" is Morton, Illinois, the same town that is home to Libby Food's pumpkin products. The state of Illinois also grows the most pumpkins in the world, harvesting around 12,300 acres of pumpkins on an annual basis.

Illinois might crank out a lot of pumpkins, but the world record holder for largest pumpkin belongs to a man from Half Moon Bay, California, by the name of Travis Gienger. Gienger grew a pumpkin in 2023 that weighed in at a massive 2,749 pounds!

Pumpkins are a native American plant and are actually a winter squash. They range in weight from a few pounds to the massive "Atlantic Giant" variety of pumpkin that can tip the scales at over 2,000 pounds.

Archaeologists excavating a tomb in Central Mexico discovered the oldest known pumpkin seeds ever found, dating back 10,000 years.

In European art of the 16th century, the pumpkin was often used as a symbol to represent the untamed wilderness of North America. Use of the pumpkin goes far back in American history. Early settlers dried pumpkin shells, cut them into strips, and wove them into mats.

In many magical traditions, pumpkins are said to represent prosperity and fertility. In parts of Mexico, they were long considered a food that gave one strength and increased endurance. They were also believed to offer protection against the cold. According to early folklore, people thought that pumpkins were a remedy for snakebites—and freckles!

According to an estimate in 2021, Americans were predicted to spend $700 million dollars on Halloween pumpkins, and the amount increases each year. If it sounds like a big number, it is, but consider this: Americans spent over $12 billion dollars on Halloween in 2023, the largest portion of which was spent on candy (about $3.6 billion).

Pumpkins are an integral part of Halloween each year. Pumpkin festivals, pumpkin carving contests, pumpkin patches, and all things pumpkin spice—which isn't really made from pumpkin—now dominate the Autumn season in the run up before Christmas.

Pumpkin carving has developed into an art all its own and there are now national and even televised competitions to see who can create the most stunning pieces of carved pumpkin art. It's a long way from the simple, smiling jack-o'-lanterns that many of us grew up with, yet, each year around Halloween thousands of traditional jack-o'-lanterns, complete with a big smile and triangle eyes, show up around homes all over the country.

While they were once used to keep people safe from various supernatural entities, jack-o'-lanterns now bring people together, and by default they function as a symbol to welcome costumed revelers and trick-or-treaters.

When you place yours out this year during the season of pumpkin spice everything, just remember, that jack on the porch may be keeping you safe from nasty wandering spirits and vampires!

Resources and Works Consulted:

Annual Report and Proceedings of the Belfast Naturalists Field Club. Ireland, 1894.

Daily News, Kingston, Ontario, Canada. "Carved Pumpkin," November 1, 1866.

"Halloween Sports and Customs," *Harper's Young People*, October 27, 1885.

Holloway, William. *General Dictionary of Provincialisms*, 1839.

Ott, Cindy. *Pumpkin: The Curious History of an American Icon*.

Haunted Houses & the Architecture of Fear

By Kevin Lee Nelson

When walking past an old abandoned mansion we sometimes pause to imagine a time when it was still occupied and we wonder: *who lived in there?* But when the moon rises over the roof, and an owl hoots from a gnarled old tree, we shudder and wonder: ***what lives in there now?*** And pick up our step.

Since childhood I have been obsessed with spooky old houses, particularly large Victorian houses that evoke a sense of mystery and wonder. Every town has at least one creepy old place that people whisper about. For me, as a young kid in Streator, IL, my first "haunted house" was the Silas Williams House, a sprawling and elaborate Queen Ann Victorian. In the early 1980s the place had definitely seen better days. I recall the overgrown yard, the two dilapidated towers, the peeling moss-colored paint, shingles missing from the roof, and a few boarded-up windows — like something right out of Scooby-Doo. It oozed a kind of sentient menace. Every time I passed by it would give me a shiver. Kids in my class (including me) would make up imaginative scary stories about what was hidden behind those walls and the strange activities of the owners. I have no idea what the actual history of the place is other than that it was built by one of the town's affluent industrialists in 1893. Probably a lot of very nice people lived there over the years, but it was the mansion's ominous and timeworn architecture that cast a spell over me. If any place was haunted, *this* was it. As a kid, the Silas Williams House became my archetypal ghost house; the yardstick by which all other haunted houses would be measured. I didn't know it at the time, but it acted as a monstrous engine powering my young imagination and inspiring a tremendous amount of creative output, and still does. It may not have been actually haunted, but it has certainly haunted my thoughts. Well over 40 years later I still have dreams about that house. The spell it cast over me still holds. Today it looks very different; mostly repaired, fresh coat of paint, and a well manicured lawn — far less sinister. I'm not disappointed, as I understand necessary restoration and regular maintenance will ensure it keeps standing for another century, and with any luck, continue to spark the imaginations of future generations of kids, and even scaring the wits out of them.

Silas Williams house today

The Style of Terror

We may not realize it, but when we close our eyes and think of a haunted house certain architectural styles will unconsciously appear in our mind's eye. Few people think of a 1960s ranch or mid-century modern home with floor-to-ceiling windows. What people *do* imagine generally falls under Victorian architecture, which includes many distinct styles: Gothic Revival, Italianate, Second Empire, Romanesque Revival, Queen Anne, Stick Style, Shingle Style, and Eastlake Style. The Victorian style began in the 1830s with Gothic Revival and continued its popularity for the next ninety years until fading around the 1920s.

Victorian homes were a huge departure from previous architectural styles in America. Prior to the Victorian era homes were designed to be symmetrical in a classical sense, like Georgian, Federal, and Greek Revival styles. That all went out the window with the Victorians. Suddenly it was fashionable to build homes that were asymmetrical and outlandish in comparison, often including towers, hexagonal bay windows, wraparound porches, and intricate details. Victorian homes were an ornate status symbol; the richer a person was, the larger and more eccentric their house became, the famous Winchester Mansion in San Jose, CA, being the most extreme expression of this philosophy. They were intentionally designed to be imposing and dominate the landscape in order to project the power and affluence of the owners. When comparing the Victorian style to earlier American architectural styles, architecture historian Sidney Robinson of the University of Chicago says, "These styles intentionally depart from clarity and comprehensibility. That's when mystery and uncertainty become possible." Unlike prior architectural styles that evoked a sense of contentment and hospitality, the Victorian style was antagonistic, formidable, and gloating — intentionally designed to project social dominance and vanity.

As all things eventually do, Victorian houses began to fall out of style, and by the 1920s the style had worn out its welcome. When compared to newer minimalistic styles, where clean lines and simplicity were the hallmark of taste, Victorians were viewed as needlessly extravagant and gaudy. In a 1934 article in the *Washington Post* a columnist called Victorian homes, "mongrel types desecrating the landscape." The new generation wanted popular modern styles, not the ornate and foreboding homes of the previous century. After all, the Gilded Age was not a prosperous time for everyone, and large, elaborate, and garish homes began to represent the divide between the haves and have-nots. Victorian houses were emblematic of rampant income inequality, political corruption, and decadent lifestyles flaunted by the elite of their grandparents' generation. They were the "McMansions" of their time. From a 20th century perspective, they were old fashioned, intimidating, gloomy, and frequently associated with childhood fears. The next generation of middle and lower class homeowners looked at those pretentious aging estates with aversion and resentment. The Victorian style became synonymous with an antiquated, grotesque, and ostentatious lifestyle. They went from being a symbol of wealth to a symbol of contempt and dread.

Victorian era homes commonly occupied large properties, but over time, as fortunes dwindled, portions of the land were often parceled off and neighborhoods and subdivisions grew around the moribund mansions. Being surrounded by modern homes made them look even more archaic and out of place. They became stereotyped and stigmatized as the brooding homes of peculiar elderly misers and deranged housebound recluses. And when eventually the money ran out, or the owners died off, the houses were abandoned, which only deepened their association with decay. Left derelict, it didn't take long for frightening stories to circulate, and they became the textbook neighborhood "haunted house."

The 1989 comedy *The Burbs* starring Tom Hanks plays on this common trope. Surrounded by well-kept modern homes and modern sensibilities, the aged, unkempt, and out-of-place Victorian "Klopek house" is a blight on the neighborhood, which is only exacerbated when strange Addams Family-esque outsiders move in and arouse suspicion and dark rumors. Every town has one of these sinister homes, or several. If an author or film director needed a location for their next Gothic novel or scary movie the familiar dilapidated Victorian home was the perfect setting that everyone could relate to.

Unfortunately, widely held attitudes of fear and neglect led to the premature demolition of thousands of 19th century houses and civic buildings. The period roughly between 50 and 80 years of age is the most perilous time for any building. After half a century buildings start to show their age, look old-fashioned, and usually require a significant amount of new investment to repair and restore them. It's between these years that many are simply torn down because they have become an expensive inconvenience or an unappreciated eye-sore. In the case of Victorian houses, all that detail work is a nightmare to keep up. During their heyday, affluent families who lived in these houses typically had staff on hand to cook, clean, and perform regular house maintenance. Keeping a large Victorian house in good shape is a full time job. That's why many were converted into boarding houses during the Great Depression, as it was the only economical way to make use of them, and little by little, the original grandeur was destroyed through regrettable conversions and remodels.

However, if a building can withstand those precarious years its chances of surviving greatly improve. After 80 years new generations start to appreciate and re-discover older styles. Trends come back around. It's similar to how most of us don't want our parents' things when they are offered to us because we grew up with all that stuff. But the opposite is true for our kids. They typically view the same items (that belonged to their grandparents or great-grandparents) as treasured heirlooms.

By the mid-1940s the haunted Victorian house had become an iconic fixture within the American mind. In 1946 *The New Yorker* published cartoonist Charles Addams' now-famous image of the ghoulish Addams Family pouring boiling oil on Christmas carolers from the tower of their spooky mansion. Their Second Empire style mansion with its characteristic tower, mansard roof, tall and narrow arched windows with shutters, iron crested widow's walk, and heavily bracketed cornices, has become the archetypal haunted house. When asked why he chose a Victorian house as the Addams Family's home, Addams said, "I LIKE Victorian houses … I'm not trying to make fun of them. I think they look better for haunts than a stone castle. I can't picture a castle musty and cracked with peeling paint." Thanks to Addams the Second Empire house became permanently associated with horror. Oddly enough, Addams himself lived in a rather unremarkable 1907 Colonial style home.

In 1960 the Second Empire style was used again and created the most recognizable spook house of them all, the Bates house in Alfred Hitchcock's classic film *Psycho*. By this time most audiences immediately associated the style with unspoken dread. Hitchcock's inspiration was Edward Hopper's now famous 1925 painting *House by the Railroad* depicting a formerly opulent Second Empire house sitting uncomfortably close to railroad tracks in an otherwise empty landscape. The forlorn house symbolizes a time that has been isolated and discarded for the sake of progress. The juxtaposition of the house and the railroad track represents the conflict between 19th-century tradition and the mobility of the 20th century, as if the past is about to be demolished by an on-coming train. Oddly enough, there is a house in my town that looks virtually identical to the Hopper painting. It too has felt the unstoppable encroachment of modernity, as a new elementary school has been built just yards away from where it stands, completely ruining the setting of the once stately house.

House by the Railroad by Edward Hopper 1925

Between the Addams Family mansion and the Norman Bates house, the Second Empire style is what most people think of when they conjure an image of a haunted house in their mind. Other horror films and series that use Second Empire houses include: *Salem's Lot, IT part I & II, Stranger Things, Monster House*, and *Beetlejuice*, just to name a few.

Another popular haunted house style is Gothic Revival. "Gothic" is a term that's often thrown round to describe any sort of dark and spooky-looking house, but Gothic Revival is a specific and distinct subset of Victorian characterized by high-pitched roofs with steep gables, pointed arches, pinnacles, elaborately carved bargeboard (what some call "gingerbread trim"), lancet windows, and sometimes, gargoyles. Traditionally Gothic buildings were constructed of stone or brick in Europe, but in America most residential buildings were constructed of wood, as it was cheap and abundant in the 19th-century. Wooden Gothic houses are a subset of Gothic Revival called "Carpenter Gothic" and also "Steamboat Gothic," the latter getting its name because they were designed to mimic the opulence and layout of steamboats of the era.

Gothic Revival houses became associated with haunted locations even earlier than Second Empire houses because of their architectural connection with European castles and old Gothic novels. Poe made his contribution early on by penning "The Fall of the House of Usher," set in a crumbing ancestral Gothic estate. In more contemporary literature, Richard Matheson's infamous Balasco House, the central character of his novel *Hell House* (1971), is described as being built in the Gothic Revival style, as can be seen in the film adaption *The Legend of Hell House* (1973). Other films that make use of Gothic Revival settings include: *The Haunting*, *The Rocky Horror Picture Show*, *Dark Shadows*, and *Crimson Peak*. Gothic Revival is immediately recognizable by its severe angles. Acutely angled gables and pointed design elements are thought to give Gothic Revival houses a "witchy" look and project an aura of mystery. It was common for many Gothic Revival homes to have Gothic Revival style furniture and decor as well, much of it characterized by uninviting pointy ornamentation. Pioneer of the Gothic Revival style, Augustus Pugin (1812-1852), once joked, "A man who remains any length of time in a modern Gothic room, and escapes without being wounded by some of its minutiae, may consider himself extremely fortunate."

Other Victorian subtypes fit the haunted look too, especially particularly eccentric examples of the Queen Anne style. Director Tobe Hooper tapped into our fears of rural degenerates and turned a decaying Folk Victorian farmhouse into a frightful abattoir in his cult classic *The Texas Chainsaw Massacre* (1974). A decrepit Folk Victorian was also used in the 2013 film *The Conjuring* to accentuate antiquity and isolation in a rural setting.

The House is Screaming

One of the biggest taboos in modern architecture is designing buildings that look anthropomorphic. It goes against everything taught in architecture or design school today. Designers and architects feel buildings should look like objects, not entities. This is because a house with a vague resemblance to a human face makes people very uncomfortable. The front door and windows can look like holes in a mask. If you walk up to a residence with upper windows situated to give the impression of eyes and a front door suggesting a yawning mouth, people will unconsciously find it unnerving. Many Victorian houses can easily give the impression of looking like a screaming face, or give the appearance of a crouching predatory animal. They can look like a presence instead of a residence. Victorian architects were either unaware of this psychological effect or they didn't care. If you want a house to look imposing and formidable, designing one that looks like it could eat you might be the way to go.

In her article, "Haunted Houses: Why old buildings scare us and modern ones don't" Chicago Tribune Architecture Critic Blair Kamin writes;

"All buildings have facades, but more than any other, the picturesque, 19th century house is a mirror of the human face. Its windows recall a pair of eyes, its front door a mouth.... When the shades are closed and a thick layer of ivy has wrapped itself around the portal, the mask seems impenetrable, and what it conceals more mysterious. And when the whole body of the house seems bent over with age, its face, too, appears transformed—into a death mask that is a palpable expression of the terror within."

One of my favorite examples of this uncanny effect is the Webster Wagner Mansion designed in 1876 by Syracuse architect Horatio Nelson White. It's a hulking monstrosity that jarringly blends Second Empire and Gothic Revival styles. Most notable are the three centrally-placed Gothic windows and the ornate porch brackets that hang down like a pair of fangs. It looks like a gigantic 3-eyed monster waiting to devour anyone who enters. The overall effect is stunningly ghastly — in a good way! Sadly, it was razed in 2016 after decades of neglect.

Yale architecture professor Kent Bloomer explores the relationship between architecture and human bodies in his book *Body, Memory, and Architecture*. Bloomer states that there is a place in our bodies somewhere near our abdomen that feels like our physical center. The same is true with houses: the first floor feels cozy, comfortable, and centered, which is akin to the gut. On the ground floor we feel sheltered, but we can also get out quickly if we need to. But the further you move up or down in a house you experience less safety and

Webster Wagner house (photo by Carl Reid via flickr)

Webster Wagner house in 1878

less comfort.

According to Bloomer the attic represents the brain. It's closest to the heavens and typically stores old items and mementos linked to memories, either fond ones or ones best forgotten. Attics are where things are hidden away and kept out of sight. In the past attics were where mad relatives, people with severe deformities, or uncontrollable children were sometimes locked away. Regarding attics, Margaret B. Vickery, PhD, director at the History of Art and Architecture Department at the University of Massachusetts Amherst says, "I think those varied spaces, with gables and dormers that break the roofline, create a somewhat mysterious silhouette and the attic spaces are easily associated with torment and haunting … Small, dark attics make us think of what could be hiding from us, and what we need to hide from; perhaps they're a metaphor for our own minds, full of places we don't want to explore." The attic is where things go to be abandoned and forgotten like childhood toys.

In the opposite direction you have the basement or cellar. It doesn't correspond to the feet, but rather the dark side of human nature. It's a home to personal demons and issues that were never entirely buried. Basements are often cold and damp — the place closet to the earth and symbolic of the grave. Basements often include confined spaces, like crawlspaces and tunnels, making them feel claustrophobic. They're also typically the most filthy place in a house, especially basements with dirt floors. They typically are dusty, cobwebbed, musty, and are prone to flood. Bloomer says, "The basement is flat out terrifying. You expect murder or some other awful things to happen there." The basement is where the bodies are buried.

A Pattern for Panic

Unlike contemporary houses with free-flowing and open-concept interiors, 19th century houses are filled with long twisting hallways and shadowed nooks and crannies. You can't see what's around the corner or hiding in the shadows, which leads to a sense of anticipation, apprehension, and unease. Low natural lighting makes spaces seem gloomy, claustrophobic, and subterranean. Heavy drapes were usually drawn to keep out sunlight and prevent it from damaging expensive furnishings. High-ceiling rooms, tall staircases, and long hallways create strange echos and weird acoustic effects. An excessive number of rooms stuffed with antique decor and crowded with ornate and uncomfortable furniture can feel isolating and create visual stress. Forced vertical perspectives, causing objects to appear closer or farther from their actual distance, creates a sense of distorted space, disorientation, and mild vertigo. As if that wasn't enough, walls were covered in dizzying patterns. Instead of calm solid colors, walls in Victorian rooms were covered in florid anxiety-inducing wallpaper from floor to ceiling as exemplified in Charlotte Perkins Gilman's classic Gothic novella, *The Yellow Wallpaper* (1892) where phantasmagoric patterns in the wallpaper eventually drive the narrator mad. Victorian homes provide all the sensory queues needed to create suspenseful and mysterious environments.

Some people were aware of these factors, even the ones who lived in them over a century ago. To mitigate the intrinsically unwholesome atmospheres of Victorian houses many owners painted the exterior in bright and vibrant colors. These became known as "painted ladies." While still rather garish, they at least looked more cheery and whimsical to passersby.

Houses that look haunted give us the creeps because it is unclear whether or not they represent a real threat. Locations that are clearly dangerous are understandable and easily avoided, but haunted houses occupy a liminal space—one foot in the physical world and one foot in the realm of the supernatural—that makes us experience a potent combination of nervousness and dread, or in today's slang, "creeped out." Compared to newer construction, older houses do present more physical danger because they were built before high safety standards and building codes were put into place. It's impossible to build a new house in a truly authentic Victorian style because it would not be up to code. As they say, *they don't build 'em like they use to*, and for good reason. Features like steep staircases, narrow hallways, confined spaces, limited exits, antiquated wiring, and combustible materials increase the potential for misfortune, not to mention toxic materials like asbestos and lead can make old houses truly hazardous. So unconsciously we know when we enter an old house we're playing by an entirely different set of rules.

It's not uncommon for old houses to have creaking floorboards, drafty windows, and bad wiring. But those often aren't the first assumptions. Because of cultural conditioning and morbid connotations with old houses, when we set foot in a Victorian house our imagination runs wild, and we immediately associate strange sounds, cold spots, and flickering lights with spectral activity. That's also their charm. Given the choice between having a murder mystery night in an old Victorian mansion or a swank contemporary "smart home," most would choose the former.

British geographer Jay Appleton hypothesized there are two crucial factors that determine whether a place is appealing or frightening to people, what he calls "prospect" and "refuge." Locations are evaluated by their level of both factors. The more of each a place offers us, the more appealing it is. "Refuge" means having a secure, protected haven that provides shelter from danger, while "prospect" refers to one's clear, unobstructed view of the surrounding landscape. Attractive places we choose to spend time in provide us with large amounts of prospect and refuge. According to Appleton, from an evolutionary standpoint they are places where "you can see without being seen, and eat without being eaten."

On the other end of the spectrum, haunted houses (or those that give the impression of being haunted), offer a grim combination of very low prospect and low refuge for us, and while at the same time offering very high refuge for things that go "bump" in the night. People interpret such environments as unsafe and dangerous. Eerie places, like old houses, also lack what environmental psychologists call "legibility." Legibility refers to how easily a place can be recognized, understood, and recalled. Simply put, inside it's a place that we can easily wander around in without getting lost. The typical haunted house is confounding, dark, full of labyrinthine passages and unexpected architectural features. Victorian house designs are notorious for their lack of legibility by keeping the line of sight as short as possible. It's not by accident that commercial faux haunted houses around Halloween do the exact same thing. Bewildering floor plans, secret rooms, and hidden staircases all create low legibility. Exteriors are similarly mystifying, as the structure's true shape is often obscured by high stone walls, wrought iron fences, overgrown vegetation, or boarded-up windows and doors.

Old houses are like fine wine; they get better with age. The older they are the more likely they are to have a bewitching history, a curious legend or two, or even an untimely death or murder within their walls. It's that aura of mystery and the macabre that draws many of us to old houses. But perhaps the gloominess and alleged supernatural phenomena is not all in our imagination.

The Victorians weren't as timid about death and the afterlife as we are today; they made it a part of their everyday life. Some houses had dedicated rooms for wakes. They would lay out dead people right in their home and people would file through to pay their last respects. It also wasn't uncommon for owners to convert their parlor, or other room, into a "seance room" to communicate with the spirits of the dead. Seances and trance mediumship were a common activity during the time of Victorian Spiritualism. People believed they were regularly opening "doorways" or "gateways" into other realms or dimensions right in their homes. Various forms of spirit contact, like mysterious knocking, inexplicable odors, possession, and even physical spirit manifestations were seen as somewhat normal occurrences among Spiritualists. Perhaps some of these portals were never properly closed, leaving an open conduit for entities to pass back and forth or become trapped within the walls of the house.

Over the years some New Age types have attempted to link hauntings to the physical composition of the haunted houses themselves, specifically their architectural design and geometry. They believe some Victorian homes are fundamentally different from other buildings and act as beacons for spirits, or innately generate an unseen negative force via occult geometry that causes despair, misfortune, and attracts malicious entities. One such person is Roger de Lafforest. In his book *Houses that Kill* (1974) he posits that certain houses can generate a harmful form of radiation he calls "negative green." According to de Lafforest this radiation (conveniently hidden somewhere along the electromagnetic spectrum and still unknown to scientists) emanates from acute angles and closed void spaces in houses, like an old well hidden under a floor. It's kind of an anti-feng shui. He claims exposure causes sickness, unease, and triggers paranormal phenomena. It's an interesting, if a bit quirky, theory, but no actual evidence exists of negative green. So-called "cancer houses," that is, houses responsible for chronic health issues for those that live in them, definitely do exist. However, it's caused by longterm exposure to toxic materials like mold and bad air in the structure, not negative green radiation.

Future Hauntings

Modern architecture exorcised the demons by introducing the "universal space" concept where space flows freely between levels. In contrast, Victorian houses compress space by dividing space into a series of small dim chambers and subliminally conjures the dark side of the human psyche. Modern and contemporary spaces may be more simplified and sunny, but there's definitely a downside. When reflecting on the soul-draining aspects of modern architecture architect Blair Kamin writes, "Clarity replaced mystery, reason supplanted romance, light replaced darkness, and the child in all of us emerged poorer for the change." He's right. Trick-or-treating at a plain boxy house with vinyl siding and picture windows doesn't have the same Halloween aesthetic as pushing through an iron gate and walking up an overgrown path to an intimidating old Victorian.

In 1956, during the height of the mid-century modern craze, a reader wrote into the Daily News-Post of Monrovia, CA, and summed it up perfectly by saying, "Modern architecture, for all its good points, has one drawback. It's hard to imagine one of those severe glass, redwood and aluminum structures as a haunted house in the same eerie way as those old Victorian monstrosities with flapping shutters. And a community without one haunted house is failing its kids." I couldn't agree more.

But where there's a will there's a way. There are a few exceptions to the familiar and ubiquitous Victorian haunted house in pop culture. Most notable is the wonderfully bizarre Ennis House designed in the Mayan Revival style by Frank Lloyd Wright. It was used as the setting for the 1959 film *The House on Haunted Hill* starring Vincent Price. Its temple-like design is the complete opposite aesthetic of Victorian architecture, though the furniture, gas chandeliers, and other decor used in the film were still distinctly Victorian — they couldn't completely go without some Victorian kitsch. Because of its utterly unique, versatile, and exotic design, the Ennis House has appeared in many other films including *Mulholland Drive, The Rocketeer, Rush Hour, Buffy the Vampire Slayer, Predator 2, Beverly Hills Cop II*, and *Blade Runner*.

Other films have followed suit. The now infamous *Amityville Horror* house (Dutch Colonial Revival circa 1925-1940) with its iconic half-moon windows is another example of how 20th century homes can become a dwelling for evil spirits. The same can be said for the contemporary mock Tudor house featured in *Poltergeist* (1982) and the vaguely Spanish Colonial style McMansion monstrosity in *Paranormal Activity* (2009). In the 1991 Wes Craven film *The People Under the Stairs*, a garden-variety Craftsman style house is revealed to be a labyrinth of secret passages and hidden traps. Even simple rustic structures can be the setting for otherworldly dangers, like the remote backwoods cabin featured prominently in the *Evil Dead* films and the misleading puzzle-box cabin from *Cabin in the Woods*. The 2012 film *Sinister* accomplished a seemingly impossible task: it made a 1960s ranch feel scary by utilizing dark nondescript interiors and capitalizing on their innate vulnerability — no place to hide. The 2022 Netflix series *Archive 81* did a remarkable job making spartan and austere mid-century Brutalist architecture, with its over-reliance on cast concrete, feel like a giant tomb. Another 2022 film, *Barbarian*, turned an outwardly innocuous suburban Airbnb into a house of horror. Lastly, the greatly underrated 2020 film *Night House* turns a seemingly innocent contemporary lake house into an inter-dimensional maze. In the film (spoiler warning) a house is designed using occult geometry to trap a demon that has been tormenting one of the characters. To make it even more interesting, there is a secret twin house hidden directly across the lake, a doppleganger house that serves as a decoy for the demon.

The doppelganger effect is another architectural feature that creates psychological unease. Have you ever driven into a neighborhood where every house on the block is a cookie-cutter duplicate? Same color, same design — all identical clones. It feels unnatural and artificial because our minds naturally want to latch onto distinct landmarks that stand out. When everything looks the same we feel lost and disoriented. Seemingly endless identical beige houses create their own unique form of suburban horror that taps into fears of uniformity and losing our identity. Duplexes also create the doppleganger effect, only on a smaller scale. While they may be space-efficient and economical, duplexes give the appearance of deformity, like a conjoined Siamese twin. They may be symmetrical and proportional, but they are functionally two separate houses fused together, unconsciously triggering deep fears many have of congenital abnormalities. So contemporary structures can certainly project terror; it just requires more work and creativity, whereas with Victorian houses it's part of their DNA. As they say, *it's a feature, not a bug*.

Going full circle back to my childhood obsession with spooky houses — I finally got one. A few years ago, I bought my dream house, an 1878 Gothic Revival that sits on the side of a small mountain overlooking my small town. It looks like the archetypal "haunted house on a hill." When I went to check it out for the first time I looked up and noticed vultures circling above the house. Not kidding. I took it as a sign because I consider vultures my spirit animal. I knew at that moment *this was the place*. It checks all the boxes. Does it loom over the town? Check. Spooky woods? Check. Overgrown yard? Check (that's me being lazy). Weird grotto? Check. Subterranean chamber? Check. Gargoyles? Check. Life goal unlocked. After a few years I still haven't noticed any ghostly activity, but who knows; maybe I'll be the one haunting it someday.

Author's 1878 Gothic Revival house, 'Buzzard Hill'

Author's Gothic library

Resources and Works Consulted:

Bailey, Dale. *American Nightmares: The Haunted House Formula in American Popular Fiction*. 1999.

Bloomer, Kent. & Charles Moore. *Body, Memory, and Architecture*. 1977.

Comaroff, Joshua. & Ong Ker-Shing. *Horror in Architecture*. 2024.

de Lafforest, Roger. *Houses That Kill*. 1974.

"Many Passing Fads," *Washington Post*. June 3, 1934.

"Haunted Houses." *Daily News-Post*. 1956.

Kamin, Blair. "Haunted Houses: Why old buildings scare us and modern ones don't." *Chicago Tribune*. Oct 31, 1993.

Patterson, Richard. *The Tragic in Architecture*. 2001.

Welcome to
Doveland
Doveland

Ghost Town Gazetteer

Doveland—The Town With No Proof It Ever Existed!

By Chad Lewis

Unlike most of the ghost towns found scattered around America, Doveland, Wisconsin, doesn't have any long-forgotten dilapidated buildings. It doesn't have any discarded vehicles rusting outside on the land where the gas station once stood. There are no old cemeteries where the founders of the town rest peacefully in the place they once loved. In fact, outside of a few vague and fuzzy testimonies from people claiming that they actually visited this odd town, Doveland seems to only have existed in our memories and the internet.

Perhaps nothing more than a creepypasta-like urban legend, the mystery of Doveland makes for the perfect fit for the Halloween edition of Ghost Town Gazetteer. How does an entire town go missing? How do people have memories of visiting a town that by all accounts never existed? This is the unbelievably fascinating tale of the town that simply disappeared from existence.

According to legend, Doveland was your typical Wisconsin small town--complete with local businesses, churches, and hard-working people who were simply trying to get by. Then, sometime in the late 1980s or early 1990s, the town completely vanished. It should be noted that in America towns disappeared all the time for a plethora of normal reasons. Many towns have been wiped out and never rebuilt due to blazing fires, devastating floods, or deadly outbreaks of infectious diseases. Oftentimes smaller towns have been annexed into their larger nearby cities. Numerous name changes have caused many once thriving towns to become forgotten relics of our past. However, in each and every instance, there was historical evidence that these towns actually existed--maps showing their location, documents recording their histories, photos capt-

-uring a moment in time. If any of these things ever existed for Doveland, they have been erased.

According to legend, the first online mention of this town occurred in 2015 with an archived but deleted Tumblr post from someone asking "Anyone here ever heard about Doveland, Wisconsin?"

So let's pretend that Doveland did exist---and if you scour the internet, you might just believe it really did. People have shared alleged photos from the 1970s and 80s that reportedly show people hanging out in Doveland businesses. Others shared images of items bearing the Doveland logo, while still others claim to have had relatives that once lived in the mysterious town. For the fun of this column let's take these claims as the gospel truth. The question then becomes---what happened to this town? This is where things get interesting and strange.

Why did Doveland disappear:

• It is another example of the Mandela Effect at work –The Mandela Effect is a social phenomenon in which a person remembers specific details of dates, names, and situations that do not align with the accepted reality. This effect received its name due to so many people having a clear memory of Nelson Mandela dying in prison during the 1980s. Just so we are all coming at this from the same reality, I am writing this column from the reality that Nelson Mandela actually died in 2013 at the ripe old age of 95.

• Doveland was swallowed up by….Fill in the blank. A black hole, an alternate dimension, extraterrestrial lifeforms, a classified government experiment, etc…Others contend that just maybe it wasn't Doveland that slipped into an alternate dimension, maybe it was all of us that shifted to somewhere/ sometime else.

• A more mundane explanation states that Doveland was the victim of Project Sanguine, a U.S. Navy project from the 1960s that looked at using extremely low frequency radio waves to better communicate with submarines. Once the project was canceled from the Upper Peninsula and Northwoods of Wisconsin, the mostly military families that lived in Doveland simply moved away. Although this explanation does nothing to explain why evidence of Doveland's existence is nowhere to be found. A more detailed telling of this explanation can be found on my friend and colleague Jeff Finup's 2023 Facebook post on Badgerland Legends.

Where does all this leave us? Is Doveland nothing more than a compelling hoax, or is there a more sinister answer at play? For the last 30-plus years, I have prided myself on traveling through nearly every inch of Wisconsin while giving over a thousand speaking engagements from all corners of the state. I can honestly say that I have no recollection of ever coming across any mention of Doveland, much less having visited it for myself. Regardless of the absurdity of this legend, I can tell you that I will certainly be keeping an eye out for this lost town on all my future travels. So, if you never hear from me again, just know that I probably became the newest resident of Doveland!

The Digital Campfire

The Backrooms

By David Weatherly

On May 12, 2019, a thread was started on the Internet site 4chan's paranormal themed message board. The original post challenged followers to put up "disquieting images that just feel off." People rose to the curious challenge and in short order, a photo was posted that caught a lot of attention. In reality, it was a simple shot, a picture of a large, vacant room with dividing walls. The room itself was innocuous. Old fluorescent lighting illuminated the space, the floor was covered with old carpet, and the entire room had a dingy, yellow tint. It was indeed an image that felt unsettling to many who saw it, even though there was no clear indication as to why it was disturbing. The day after the photo was up, an anonymous user posted a comment that expressed a creepy possibility:

"If you're not careful and you noclip out of reality in the wrong areas, you'll end up in the Backrooms, where it's nothing but the stink of old moist carpet, the madness of mono-yellow, the endless background noise of fluorescent lights at maximum hum-buzz, and approximately six hundred million square miles of randomly segmented empty rooms to be trapped in. God save you if you hear something wandering around nearby, because it sure as hell has heard you."

Thus began the mythology of the Backrooms.

To clarify things up for those not familiar with the term— "noclip" or "noclipping"—originated among the video game community. It was first used to describe a glitch in a video game that allowed a player character to pass through supposedly solid surfaces like walls. The term is now applied to what some believe is a real life possibility—stepping outside of the normal boundaries of the world and into something much stranger—another reality—one that is a disturbing and dangerous place.

The original Backrooms photograph

Noclipping can be, and usually is, unintentional. According to popular lore, a person might noclip due to intense stress or confusion. Some people say it occurs due to a simple twist of fate, one that causes an innocent person to step into another dimension, one well outside of our own world.

The Backrooms have become firmly connected to the idea of noclipping and it's not a place that people are meant to be wandering about. There's a unique sense of dread about the Backrooms and beyond the vacant corridors and rooms "things" lurk about, things that you don't want to encounter.

The photograph, along with the short paragraph posted the following day, proved to be the beginning of an ever-evolving mythology created by the collective efforts of countless people who have connected online to talk and write about the Backrooms.

The topic quickly moved from 4chan to Reddit and eventually to other social media platforms and the Backrooms morphed from a Creepypasta into a full blown cooperative horror mythology that has branched off in multiple directions.

Interest in the Backrooms got another spike when a young man named Kane Parsons created a video set in the maze-like world. The short horror production went viral online and led to a YouTube series made by Parsons. The video series proved so popular that the A24 production company optioned a film adaptation of the concept which is set to be directed by Parsons himself. The film will take the horror of the Backrooms to a larger, mainstream audience.

But what was it that people found so disturbing about the idea of the Backrooms to begin with? Interestingly the Backrooms have dovetailed into another concept that has garnered a lot of attention online—the liminal space aesthetic.

The Merriam-Webster Dictionary defines liminal as "of, or relating to, or being an intermediate state, phase, or condition: In-between, transitional."

By their nature, liminal states have a mysterious, otherworldly quality. For instance, the time when day becomes night, or the time between being awake and asleep when you question what's real and what's a dream.

In terms of the liminal space aesthetic, especially the Backrooms, the idea has taken on an even darker context and represents the feeling that something is truly wrong or distorted within a space that *should* be seen as normal. Sometimes this can be as simple as a space with a defined function that's outside of its usual boundaries. Imagine, for instance, finding yourself alone in a high school late at night. The hallways, the classrooms, the gym and cafeteria are all empty. There are posters on the walls, papers on the desk…all the typical signs of the building's regular use, and yet, at that moment, it is strangely quiet and vacant. It does, at the least, feel strange for the average person and downright terrifying for others. Our minds, after all, expect the normal activity and our brains try to fill in what's missing, even though we know logically that it's after hours and outside of the routine time for activity.

Plenty of horror movies have used such settings with slashers or monsters lurking in what should be a normal and safe space. In some situations, a long hallway can become frightening when one is forced to wonder what's at the end and just around the corner. Transformed by the unknown, the odd sense of the space itself sends a chill up the spine.

Some people argue that the liminal space aesthetic began with the Backrooms. Whatever the case, the online horror lore has certainly added to the interest in depictions of liminal space.

In an article for *Musee Magazine,* writer Karl Emil Koch refers to liminal space as:

"A type of emotional space that conveys a sense of nostalgia, lostness, and uncertainty. They often lack activity and purpose either because they lay unused or because they are spaces of transition—of becoming instead of being. They connect to the basic human condition of ephemerality, the notion that nothing lasts forever. As generic as liminal spaces are, they become impossible to locate and thus transcend time and place, attaining an eerie, otherworldly feeling."

One Room or Many?

The growth of the Backrooms lore unfolded in a fashion similar to the Slenderman mythos. Since its inception, there have been so many contributors to the shared mythos that it has branched off in many directions. The big difference, of course, is that while the Slenderman is a singular entity, the Backrooms have a much wider scope, hence, there is more potential for complexity and variation.

Some writers have posed the idea that the world of the Backrooms consists of multiple levels with the original Backrooms being one of the many levels. Each space has its own unique and disturbing aspects. For instance, one level is plagued by the sounds of machinery, another is haunted by the cries and whispers of lost souls, while yet another level is filled with predators who watch and wait for their next unwitting victim.

Some writers have added even more complex levels—there's one that's an endless maze of service tunnels and another that is a weird library filled with endless volumes of forbidden or long lost lore.

By some accounts, each level is more distorted and farther from our everyday normal reality and as such, they are successfully harder and harder to navigate.

Then there are the monsters. A number of entities that prowl the Backrooms have been identified. There are the "smilers," strange figures who always observe from a distance. Silent and creepy, the smilers only watch—maintaining a creepy smile the entire time. Although they haven't been known to attack anyone, their true intent remains veiled, and people doubt that they are truly benign creatures.

Then there are the "skin-stealers." With a name like that it doesn't take much imagination to know what their intentions are. The skin-stealers are vicious and aggressive predators who are constantly on the hunt.

The mythology of the Backrooms has grown and expanded so much that there's a division among those who participate in the building of the lore. Some people fiercely adhere to the "True Backrooms," and support the original concept of the place and the idea that there is only one level, albeit an incredibly vast one. This concept is seen as a more streamlined version of the Backrooms and leaves a lot of room for an individual to "fill in the blanks." In the world of the True Backrooms, the horrors tend to be unseen and just out of view. This plays closer to the concept of the terrifying boogeyman—dangerous—but just out of sight. It makes sense in some ways, after all, an individual's mind can create horrors that another person simply wouldn't conceive of in the same way. Whatever version one adheres to, the Backrooms are a disturbing place.

Roots and Influences

PC Gamer magazine compared the various levels of the Backrooms to author H.P. Lovecraft's R'lyeh, a strange lost city from the writer's Cthulhu mythos. Lovecraft describes the city as "built in measureless eons behind history by the vast, loathsome shapes that seeped down from the dark stars."

The magazine also draws comparisons between The Backrooms and the setting of a Japanese manga series named *Blame!* The manga is set in an "immense megastructure that continues to be built as an AI's approximation of what a city should look like, long after humanity has been all but extinguished." The city includes nonsensical geometry and large, empty chambers. Imagine an M.C. Escher drawing come to life.

While the setting of The Backrooms is modern, one can't help but see the various older influences that have played into the creation of the shared world. The maze-like passages, filled with hidden dangers, harkens to the Greek tale of the labyrinth—an elaborate, confusing maze built for King Minos of Crete. The labyrinth, or course, held the monstrous minotaur, a half man, half bull that killed those it found wandering in its lair.

When I first heard about the Backrooms, my initial thought was the link to the Twilight Zone. Reading through the concepts of the weird, endless space, one can almost hear Rod Serling's voice:

"There is a fifth dimension beyond that which is known to man. It is a dimension as vast as space and timeless as infinity. It is the middle ground between light and shadow, between science and superstition, and it lies between the pit of man's fears and the summit of his knowledge."

Obviously, Serling was talking about his creation the Twilight Zone, but the statement could just as easily apply to the modern Backrooms, and the writer was certainly talking about the liminal space aesthetic well before it was a popular topic online.

While the Backrooms has obvious similarities to these earlier concepts and stories, the lore has also swept in more modern ideas such as the "glitch in the matrix" concept—the idea that we are living in some kind of simulation and that there may be another reality just outside of our perception, one that's run by someone, or something else.

Finding The Backrooms

From the time it was posted in 2019, the physical location where the original Backrooms photo was taken remained a mystery. Some people even thought that the image was photoshopped or created using a computer program. In May 2024, however, the location of the photo was discovered—it turned out to be a retail space in Oshkosh, Wisconsin.

The news came from someone writing under the username @tjxz-z and was announced on the social media website X. The writer reported that a friend had found the source of the original Backrooms photo. According to the online archive the *Wayback Machine*, the picture was taken in 2002 at the site of a former furniture store in Oshkosh. The furniture store had closed, and the space had been acquired by the Oshkosh RC cars team. In 2002, the RC car group was in the process of remodeling the space and converting it to use for RC tracks.

As it turned out, when the furniture store was in business, they had partitions and false walls inside the space. Since they had been in operation for some time, when they moved out, the interior needed some serious updating—the lights were old, the wallpaper yellowing, and the carpet was well worn. The new business completely refurbished and updated the space, and it now looks nothing like it did in the original Backrooms photo. That photo by the way, was taken as the new occupants were starting their remodel, possibly as part of a before and after photo set.

On a final curious note, while the Backrooms are a fictional world built online, there are people who have reported stepping outside of reality, the glitch in the matrix as mentioned previously, or the experience of a "time-slip" wherein they find themselves in some other time and/or place. In some ways, this could be considered "noclipping."

With the power of belief and the collective consciousness, who knows, perhaps someone may slip out of our reality and noclip into a long maze of endless spaces. Best hope it doesn't happen to you.

Resources and Works Consulted:

Koch, Karl Emil. "The Cult Following of Liminal Space," *Musee Magazine*, November 2, 2020.

Lovecraft, H.P. "The Call of Cthulhu," *Weird Tales*, February 1928.

Merriam-Webster Dictionary online.

Wickens, Katie. "Noclipping Is No Joke: The Strange World of The Backrooms Explained." *PC Gamer Magazine*, July 7, 2022.

The Ghoul: From Ancient Arabia to Today

By Kevin Lee Nelson

In contemporary American culture the term "ghoul" is commonly used as a generic catch-all term referring to zombies, vampires, or other types of undead fiends. It's also used to describe living individuals involved in morbid and macabre activities. For example, grave robbers, cannibals, and necrophiliacs are frequently described as *ghoulish,* though the term is also used on less offensive types, like ambulance chasers, morticians, members of the goth subculture, and folks who enjoy gallows humor. When we think of ghouls we often picture a creepy disheveled person with a deathly pallor lurking around a gloomy graveyard — perhaps gnawing on a bone that looks suspiciously human. This is how we characterize ghouls today; however, our contemporary concept is a distortion of how ghouls were represented historically. After over three-hundred years of the folkloric telephone game, today's ghouls in Western culture are almost unrecognizable from their ancient predecessors.

But what is the origin of the ghoul, and where did the mythology originate? Even though ghoul folklore is found throughout Western culture, tales of ghouls can be traced back over two thousand years to a pre-Islamic Mesopotamian origin. Throughout North Africa and the Middle East, from Morocco to Afghanistan, ghūls were a type of *jinn,* or evil spirit, that lived in the desert. Fittingly, the word *ghūl* (later anglicized to "ghoul") is derived from the Arabic word *ghala,* meaning "to seize," or *ghal,* "kill." While most ghouls were female (sometimes called *Ghouleh*), the male counterparts are sometimes called *Qutrub,* meaning "madman" or "drugs," referring to the state of delirium experienced when lost in the desert.

Ghūls played an important, though dreadful, part of desert culture. Even the star Algol (*Al-Gol,* the demon) is named after this fearsome creature. They were described in different, and sometimes contradictory, ways depending on particular cultural or regional beliefs, but generally speaking, ghūls were shape-shifting female enchantresses, or devils, that preyed upon travelers in remote areas. In their natural form they were ugly creatures, often hairy, and walked on cloven feet. It was said that ghūls were so horrifying they would cause most men to faint on the spot. However, they had the power to transform into attractive women (except for the tell-tale cloven feet) in order to seduce travelers and lead them astray into the desert, leading to their death. Once a traveler was isolated, packs of ghūls would attack them and devour them. Ghūls would confuse travelers in the desert by causing them to lose their sense of direction. In the desert, losing one's bearings can be deadly. If the ghūls didn't get them, the desert did.

English traveler Charles Montagu Doughty (1843–1926), in his work *Travels in Arabia Deserta of 1888*, mentions an Arab Bedouin who swore that he saw a "*ghroˆl*" or a "*ghruˆ l*" in the desert. The man states, "the sex is only feminine, she has a foot as the ass' hoof, and a foot as an ostrich. She entices passengers, calling to them over the waste by their names, so that they think it is their own mother's or their sister's voice. . . ." One may notice similarities between traditional ghouls and other deceiver demons and monstrous enchantresses found throughout European mythology like sirens, harpies, nymphs, lamia, rusalka, and succubi.

Ghūl from the Persian epic ***Shahnemeh***

Another nineteenth century English traveler, Edward Westermarck, claimed that a malevolent she-ghoul called "Aysha Qandı¯sha" was known to prey upon men in the region of Morocco. Her one vulnerability was that she was afraid of iron. He further elaborated, saying, "She appears in various shapes, now as a child, now as a grown-up woman, with long hair and beautiful face, but with the legs of a goat or an ass. She knows the name of every man; but when she calls anybody he should not answer her, for she is very dangerous. Not only does she kill men, she is, also, sometimes said to eat them."

Through the centuries people throughout North Africa and Arabia had a strong belief in the existence of ghouls. One Beduin myth mentions how ghouls came to be. They believed that when the devils wanted to eavesdrop on Heaven, God threw meteors at them. Some were hit and fell into the sea, becoming crocodiles, while others were smashed to the ground and changed into ghouls. This is why jinn in general are associated with the desert and the elements of wind and fire. Ghouls were known to light fires in the desert to lure travelers into dangerous areas and lead them astray. In some ways their fires were similar to Western folk tales of the will-o'-the-wisp; that is, mysterious spook lights that lead careless travelers into treacherous swamps and deadly quagmires. Ghoul fires serve a similar function in the desert after nightfall.

These were not just stories to frighten small children; stories of ghouls were taken very seriously throughout Middle Eastern history, and the reality of ghouls was not questioned. Even today it's not uncommon for people to believe in the existence of ghouls and other types of jinn. It is believed they are able to shape-shift into animals, particularly hyenas. Besides their ability to shape-shift, ghouls were dangerous because they were difficult to kill. Legends state that bullets do not harm them. One of the only ways to kill a ghoul is by a single stroke of a sword. If more than one strike is required it would never die until one thousand blows followed. For example, in Richard Burton's translation of the "Story of Prince Sayf Al-Muluk and the Princess Badi'a Al-Jamal" a man and his companions are captured by a male ghoul and taken back to its cave. Before they could be killed and eaten they fight back and slash the ghoul with a sword, a single stroke across its waist. Then the ghoul cries out, "O man, thou desire to slay me, strike me a second stroke." As the man is about to strike it again, his companion says, "Smite him not a second time, for then he will not die, but will live and destroy us."

Ghouls in Western Culture

The first reference to ghouls in Europe was in Barthelemy d'Herbelot's (1625–1695) *Bibliothe`que orientale, ou Dictionnaire universel, contenant tout ce qui fait connaı^tre les peuples de l'Orient* (1697), considered to be the first encyclopedia of Islam written in a European language. The entry for the "Goul" describes it as the most fearful kind of jinn. Just a few decades later, ghouls became popularized in the Western world though literature, specifically by Antoine Galland (1646–1715) and his translation of the *Arabian Nights* into

French (twelve volumes, 1704–17), a classic collection of Middle Eastern folktales compiled in Arabic during the Islamic Golden Age. The English language translation was titled *One Thousand and One Nights*. Galland took considerable liberties with his translation. In fact, many critics consider it more of an adaptation than a true translation. For example, Galland stripped the supernatural and demonic side from the Arabic ghoul away and transformed them into more mundane creatures that feast on corpses in cemeteries. While still frightful, they were stripped of their magical nature, reducing them to near-mindless graveyard-dwelling cannibals, not the cunningly wicked deceivers they once were. It's very telling that the ghoul's alleged preference for sepulchral haunts and necrophagic appetites are not mentioned anywhere throughout Arabic language, literature, culture, or folktales. This indicates that Galland added these embellishments himself, presumably to make the ghoul's description seem more horrific and gruesome for readers. Yet it's these exact characteristics, inaccurate as they are, that have defined the ghoul in Western culture for over three centuries.

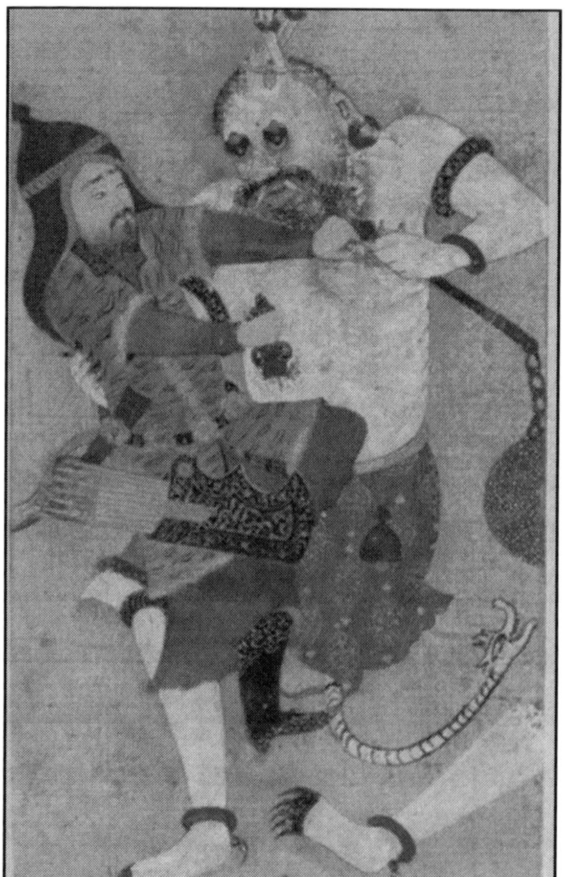

The Ghoul King attacking Rostam from the ***Shahnemeh***

European and American writers were greatly influenced by *Arabian Nights* and its exotic portrayal of Middle Eastern mythology. But it was tales involving ghouls that really resonated with writers who had a penchant for the macabre. English novelist William Beckford wrote *Vathek* (1786), an Arabian Gothic novel that includes a race of subhuman ghouls. Beckford was directly inspired by Galland's French translation of *Arabian Nights*, as he used the French spelling and connotation of the word 'goule' just as it appeared in the text. In *Vathek* ghouls are described as pale and haggard human-looking beings with a strange and garbled manner of speech.

They live in abandoned tombs and beneath cemeteries where they can easily feed upon recently interred corpses.

Hans Christian Andersen borrowed the mythology of ghouls in his literary fairy tale, "The Wild Swans" (1838). In one scene the heroine Eliza has to pass a group of ghouls feasting on a corpse. Ten years later Edgar Allan Poe mentions ghouls in his poem "The Bells" (1848), describing them as "the people, they that dwell up in the steeple" tolling the bells and reveling in the depressive effect upon those that hear the melancholy bells. Poe says, "They are neither man nor woman— / They are neither brute nor human— / They are Ghouls." Poe's 1847 poem "Ulalume" also references a "ghoul-haunted woodland of Weir."

Sketch by H.P. Lovecraft of his vision of ghoul from ***Pickman's Model*** *1934*

Celebrated horror writer H.P. Lovecraft helped popularize the ghoul in American culture after his tale "Pickman's Model" appeared in the October issue of *Weird Tales* in 1927. In the story a young eccentric painter living in Boston's North End gains notoriety after exhibiting his horrifically realistic paintings of ghouls. The story ends with the narrator discovering they were not painted from the artist's imagination at all, but modeled after actual creatures that lived under the city's cemeteries. The tale has been adapted to television and film a number of times, including a 1972 episode of *Night Gallery*, and most recently in a 2022 episode of Guillermo del Toro's *Cabinet of Curiosities*, starring Crispin Glover and Ben Barnes.

Lovecraft's ghouls are somewhat similar to Arabic ghouls, as they share a humanoid shape with cloven feet. Where they depart from traditional ghouls is how they're described as dog-faced graveyard scavengers that live in subterranean tunnels beneath burial grounds and feed on human remains. He states they are "seldom completely human, but often approached humanity in varying degree. Most of the bodies, while roughly bipedal, had a forward slumping, and a vaguely canine cast. The texture of the majority was a kind of unpleasant rubberiness."

Fantasy and horror writer Clark Ashton Smith proposed a unique hypothesis regarding how ghouls reproduce and survive. In the tale "The Nameless Offspring", published in the June 1932 issue of *Strange Tales of Mystery and Terror*, Smith states that ghouls procreate by mating with women who are mistakenly buried alive. Premature burial was a shockingly common occurrence in the past. The ghouls hear the struggle and screams of the person mistakenly buried, dig them up, and mate with them. Presumably the ghoul gene is dominant, as the offspring is a ghoul abomination. Additionally, Lovecraft addressed how ghouls remained a viable subspecies in "Pickman's Model" by mixing ghoul lore with Celtic changling lore. He states that ghouls steal human babies and replace them with their own ghoul-babies to maintain genetic diversity. Once the ghoul child matures they realize they're not entirely human and seek out their graveyard-dwelling brethren. Secret baby-swapping is a key part of the changling myth. Folklorists speculate that in the past it was a way for people to explain autism and infant illnesses that affect the brain. Saying a baby was stolen and replaced by a changeling explained why a baby that seemed normal at first, suddenly seems different and has developmental problems.

Counterparts in the Americas

A somewhat similar creature in American folklore to the original Arabic ghūl is a creature from Pennsylvania lore called the *Giwoggle*. The legends go back to roughly the 1870s. They are described as around six feet tall, wolf-like, with the hands of a bird and the cloven feet of a horse. Giwoggles are summoned by witches to harass their enemies by frightening farm animals, spreading sickness, and vandalizing property by trampling crops and damaging equipment. Their mixed-up body parts were intended to confuse and disorient trackers in the wilderness. Would-be pursuers begin following hoof tracks, but after a bit the tracks mysteriously stop, only to be continued on by large bird tracks. This is somewhat similar to another American mythical beast known as the Tote-Road Shagamaw, native to the Northwoods, that alternates between walking on cloven hooves and bear paws. (See vol. 1 of *Back Roads Lore* for more information on the Tote-Road Shagamaw.)

Of course, wherever you have monsters you have those that hunt them. Local nineteenth-century folk hero and professional monster-hunter, Isaac Gaines, better known as "Loop Hill Ike," was the grandson of an escaped slave from Virginia and was renowned throughout Clinton County, PA, for battling witches, ghosts, and especially giwoggles. He lived in the Keating area from 1837 to 1915. Today giwoggles are the official monster of Clinton County.

Perhaps the most analogous counterpart to the Arabic ghūl is the Deer Woman, or Deer Lady, of Native American lore. She is a vengeful shape-shifting spirit known among the Lakota, Ojibwe, Cherokee, and many other tribes. Deer Woman seeks out men who have harmed women or children or that have been unfaithful to their partners. Like the Arabic ghoul, she has hoofed feet (like a deer). Similarly, she seduces men by appearing as an attractive young woman and lures them to their death. Men become entranced with her beauty and lose all interest in everything, even self preservation. All they can think of is her. Eventually they starve to death, or waste away. Deer Woman serves as a kind of bogey*woman* to keep girl-crazy young men in line and also serves as a warning for those who would mistreat women.

In Mexican and Central American folklore there is a ghoul-like creature called *La Siguanaba* (sometimes also *Cegua*, *La Sihuehuet*, or *Cigua*). The etymology of the name has its origin in indigenous languages and loosely means "net-woman", as she seduces and ensnares men. La Siguanaba is described as a shape-shifting spirit that often takes the form of an attractive long-haired woman when seen from behind. Like the Arabic ghūl, she lures men away into danger. In Central America men are usually lured into deep canyons or dark forests until they become lost. When her face is finally revealed it is the face of a horse, or sometimes a skull. Once her face is revealed men either die of fright on the spot or go mad. La Siguanaba can also imitate the appearance of a man's girlfriend or wife, at least from the back. When La Siguanaba appears to children she takes on the appearance of the child's mother. She will lure the children into the wilderness until they are lost. Once she touches the children, they are driven insane, and she abandons them to die alone.

In South America there is the legend of *Patasola*, meaning "one leg." She is a shape-shifter demon of the jungle that appears as a betutiful young woman. She appears at the edge of the jungle to male hunters, loggers, miners, and animal herders and lures them into the jungle where they become hopelessly lost. Once they are disoriented she reveals her true and hideous form. She is described as having only one breast, bulging eyes, catlike fangs, and a hooked nose. But her most notable feature is that she only has a single leg with a cloven hoof. After her frightful nature is revealed she devours her victims. Patasola is sometimes seen as a protector of the jungle and is unforgiving to men, like loggers, who are destructive to her domain.

Deer Woman

Ghoulish Evolution

In Western culture the contemporary ghoul shares some similarities with the classic ghūl of Arabia, particularly their cloven hooves. Yet in other ways they have changed considerably. Often contemporary ghouls are mostly hairless, have pale or grayish skin, pointed ears, and powerful claws for digging. Most depictions of ghouls include heavy, elongated, canine-like jaws (perfect for crushing bones, I suppose). They usually prefer to east corpses, whereas traditional ghouls preferred killing and eating live human beings. Additionally, modern ghouls are entirely flesh-and-blood and not of a magical or spiritual nature at all, more animal than demon. Instead of haunting isolated deserts, mountains, and ruins they now exclusively inhabit cemeteries and catacombs. Instead of devious creatures masquerading as beautiful women they are gangling half-witted beasts that attack with brute force and not through sly subterfuge.

Ghouls continue evolving within popular culture. Interestingly, in George A. Romero's classic horror film *Night of the Living Dead* (1968) the reanimated corpses were originally referred to as "ghouls." However, the media and the public kept calling them "zombies" and the term stuck. If this twist of fate hadn't happened we'd likely refer to today's zombie films and shows like *The Walking Dead* as part of the "Ghoul Apocalypse" genre instead of the Zombie Apocalypse genre.

One of the newer pop-culture interpretations of ghouls is the semi-undead thrall character. Ghouls frequently play the role of daytime protectors of vampires. They are seen as semi-human servants that are in league with their vampire master. Sometimes they are half-vampire and able to walk out in the daylight. Other times they are in a supernatural creature class of their own, yet subservient to vampires. A prime example of this breed is the ghoul played by Billy Cole in the cult vampire film *Fright Night* (1985). His character serves as a bodyguard and right-hand of the main protagonist vampire played by Chris Sarandon. Cole's ghoul is stronger than a normal human, impervious to bullets, and not constrained by the daylight, but he's not as strong as his master and has seemingly little free will of his own. The servant/thrall ghoul concept was further reinforced and formalized by the role-playing game *Vampire: The Masquerade*, in addition to a myriad of contemporary horror novels.

Another recent literary invention suggests that ghouls are able to shapeshift into the form of the last victim they devoured (alive or dead). Additionally, it has been suggested in various forms of media that ghouls of this variety can also access the memories of the person they consumed by eating their brain, allowing them to blend into society by impersonating their victim. This feeds into contemporary fears of impostors and clones, as popularized by *Invasion of the Body Snatchers*.

Ghouls continue playing a role in pop culture and have recently appeared in the Netflix horror-thriller miniseries *Ghoul* (2018). Ghouls also made an appearance in the popular TV show *Supernatural* as living monsters that could only be killed by decapitation. Additionally, there is a popular manga graphic novel series called *Tokyo Ghoul* where a title character gets bit by a ghoul and becomes half ghoul – half human. In the series ghouls look just like regular people, but they like to eat human flesh. Even more recently, Amazon's post-apocalyptic *Fallout* series (based on the popular *Fallout* video game) has a character called "The Ghoul" (played by Walton Goggins), a callous gunslinger mutated by a mysterious drug. The drug extends his life and helps him cheat death, but it has a serious side-effect; it turns him into a living zombie. Even children's cartoons have used the ghoul trope. The *Groovie Goolies* (1970) was an animated series about a group of hip monsters that played in a rock band.

The nature and appearance of the ghoul will continue to evolve with culture; of that we can be sure, much like how vampires have evolved from their hideous tomb-dwelling ancestors into beautiful, well-dressed, heart-throbs. But that doesn't mean the original ghūls of the ancient world have completely vanished. Just remember, if you're traveling alone in some remote area and a beautiful woman offers to give you directions, make sure you ask to see her feet first before heading off in that direction.

Resources and Works Consulted:

Al-Rawi, Ahmed K. "The Arabic Ghoul and its Western Transformation." *Folklore* Vol. 120, No. 23. December 2009.

———. "The Mythical Ghoul in Arabic Culture." *Cultural Analysis* #8. 2009.

Beckford, William. *Vathek*. 1816.

Connors, Scott. "The Ghoul." In *Icons of Horror and the Supernatural*. 2006.

Egerkrans, Johan. *The Undead*. 2018

"Ghoul Snake Inhabits Cemetery." *Logansport Journal*. September 3, 1889.

"Graveyard Ghoul." *Galion Inquirer*. 1884.

Lebling, Robert. *Legends of the Fire Spirits: Jinn and Genies from Arabia to Zanzibar*. 2011.

Lovecraft, H.P. "Pickman's Model." *Weird Tales*. October 1927.

Smith, Clark Ashton. "The Nameless Offspring." In *The Abominations of Yondo*. 1960.

Wetmore, Kevin J. Jr. *Eaters of the Dead: Myths and Realities of Cannibal Monsters*. 2021.

The Folklore of Bats
By David Weatherly

Along with black cats, bats are one of the animals most frequently associated with Halloween. They're a common part of seasonal art and decorations, filling the sky with their distinctive forms. But when and how did bats become associated with the holiday? The roots of these connections run deep. Many people believe the bat connection to the holiday goes all the way back to Halloween's roots and the Celtic celebration of Samhain.

The holiday marked the end of summer and the harvest season, and the beginning of the dark half of the year. At this time, it was believed that the spirits of the dead would rise and walk the land. As part of their celebration, and as a way to ward off any vengeful spirits that might come around, the Celts built large bonfires.

Now, anyone who's been camping knows that bonfires can attract insects, which in turn attract bats. Modern researchers assume this would have been the case in ancient times and that the Celts would have seen the bats zipping around at the edge of the fire and believed that they were the spirits of the dead. We don't really know if this was the case, and the idea is a bit fanciful. It also assumes that early people wouldn't have understood the nature of bats, yet we know they did.

Nate Fuller, a member of Boston University's bat biology program, posed a much more likely theory to explain how bats ended up being associated with Halloween. Fuller references Irish and Scottish immigrants who came to the United States in the 1800s and brought their traditions and celebrations with them, including their holiday Samhain. Since so many of these immigrants were living in the northeast, they would have seen large numbers of bats moving about in the fall as the animals began their migration south for the winter. Thus, bats would have been noted as a sign of the season and connected to Halloween.

On a practical level, this makes a lot of sense. Even today, bonfires and campfires are common in the fall and as a result, more people tend to see bats flying about.

Still, bats have a lot of supernatural connections and not surprisingly, there's a large body of folklore around the creatures that dates back to the ancient world. In Ancient Greece and Rome, it was believed that placing the figure of a bat under a pillow would prevent sleep. This may have been linked to the nocturnal nature of bats. Bats have long been connected to the occult and the spirit world and have been associated with initiation and transformation. In some traditions even seeing a bat is said to be a message that a transformation is about to take place in one's life.

There's also a lot of folkloric sayings that link bats and the weather. Some of them are general, such as bats flying late in the evening indicate that fair weather is on the way.

There's also bat lore associated with specific places or professions. For instance, if bats live in a theater, and fly over the stage during a rehearsal, it means that the play is a guaranteed success.

In general, bats flying into a building or home can mean a wide range of things. Sometimes the lore is very specific. For example, according to an old belief, if a bat showed up around your home on Halloween it meant that your house was haunted.

Still, there's a lot of superstitions connected to bats that foretell doom or misfortune in some manner. Bats flying into a house or building could mean that someone inside was going to go insane, go blind, or go missing the following day. A bat flying in could also mean that bad news was soon coming.

If all of these misfortunes aren't enough, we have to consider that there's a lot of folklore involving bats and death.

Death Omens

Bats have long been considered omens and in general, bats showing up around a person or their home has long thought to be an indication of death. Of course, the interpretation of these omens varies greatly depending on time period or location. Even the behavior of the bat when it's inside has a bearing on how the omen is interpreted.

A general superstition that's found in many places says that if a bat flies around your head three times, it's predicting death. Apparently, there's no use running inside because if it circles your house three times, it's also an omen of death.

Being the melting pot that it is, a lot of folklore from around the world has ended up in the United States, in large part due to immigration over the years. As groups of immigrants from different countries settled in America, they brought their traditions and superstitions with them, so we find a wide range of bat lore around North America, some of which varies greatly.

In Europe, a bat entering the home was believed to be a forewarning that a death was coming, and this belief is found in parts of the United States even today. Jewish and German immigrants say that a bat in the attic foretells the death of someone in the home.

In parts of Illinois, if a bat gets in your house and stays too long, it means that a death is going to take place in the home. If the bat leaves soon after it enters, the death will be that of a relative.

In New Mexico, a bat in the house means that someone will die in eight days. If you're in a midwestern state, you've got longer to get your affairs in order since a bat in the house foretells death in one to six months. According to lore from Washington state, you've got even more time—a full year before the end comes.

In western New York, a couple of things have to be in sync for the omen to foretell death. A bat has to fly around your house—while a dog is howling—to mean doom.

Occasionally, there are measures mentioned that will cancel the coming death. Consider Nova Scotia. Bats entering a home there are a bad omen in general. If the creature lands on something while it's inside, it means the man of the house will soon die. If the bat doesn't land on anything but keeps flying around, it means the woman of the family will soon perish. If there's a sick person in the home, they're the one who will soon die. BUT all of this death can be avoided by throwing a handful of salt into the fire.

BRITISH BATS AT HOME.

Bats flying down the chimney also reportedly foretell a death in the house, but people in Arkansas have a proactive measure to avoid such misfortunes; they say putting a horseshoe in the fireplace will scare bats away. Arkansas natives can't escape all bat related misfortunes; they say that just dreaming about a bat flying into your house is bad news and in this case it's symbolic that a dear friend will soon pass away.

Good Luck/Bad Luck

A lot of bat folklore seems contradictory and truthfully it would be impossible to follow all of the superstitions even if you wanted to. Here are some other common bat connected beliefs:

Seeing bats flying around in the early evening sky is believed to signal that there's fine weather ahead, but if a bat flies into a building, rain is likely on the horizon. Seeing bats flying outside may mean good weather, but if the bats are crying, they symbolize bad luck.

Seeing a bat means that something good is about to happen, but spotting a bat during daylight hours brings a dose of bad luck. If a bat falls on you, you'll have a stroke of good luck. Just don't bring the bat into your house, doing so is an ill omen and portends the death of someone in the family.

If a bat flies close to a person, it means the individual will soon be betrayed. A bat flying into a house may mean that the people inside will soon leave the residence.

If a bat comes into your room and lands on something for even a moment, it's a sign of good fortune. It's also a symbol of good luck if a bat enters your home and hangs on the ceiling in the kitchen.

If a bat swoops in during a wedding ceremony—you guessed it—it's a bad omen for the marriage and it may mean that forces from the spirit world are getting involved.

If a bat flies around your house three times—it's an ill omen. In Italy, the mere presence of a bat could bring about fits and convulsions.

There's a lot of folklore that involves using various parts of bats, be it their blood, hearts or wings. In some instances, carrying, wearing, or otherwise using some of the animals' body parts was believed to bring some kind of luck or protection. Since it wasn't so lucky for the poor bat, one wonders why people thought such things were so effective. Fortunately, people have mostly moved beyond such ideas and in many cases such things would be illegal since a lot of bat species are on the endangered list.

Conversely, in many traditions, killing a bat brings about bad luck. Some lore says that killing a bat will shorten the life of the person who does the deed. (This should have been passed on to all the people who thought taking body parts from a bat would bring them good luck!)

It's also bad luck to kill a bat that has entered your room, and doing so means that you will soon die yourself.

If you're wondering where all the doom and gloom around bats came from, much of it goes back to Europe and the fear of the devil.

Witches' Birds

In Medieval Europe, bats were commonly associated with witches and witchcraft and many people thought that they were witches' familiars. Bats, it was thought, could carry messages to and from the devil.

It was also commonly believed that witches used the blood of bats as an ingredient when making their flying ointment. Blood from the animals was also purportedly used in other magical brews and potions.

Shakespeare even incorporated this into his play Macbeth when his three witches added "Eye of newt and toe of frog, wool of bat and tongue of dog" to their potion. The bard also mentioned bats in The Tempest Act 1, Scene 2, when the character Caliban placed a curse on his master Prospero, which included the line "All the charms of Sycorax, toads, beetles, bats, light on you!"

During the Middle Ages, Christians first started associating bats with evil forces. They were seen as dark, unclean animals and according to the Old Testament, they are among the animals that the "people of God" are not allowed to eat (Leviticus 11:19 and Deuteronomy 14:18).

When Dante wrote his epic *Inferno*, he further solidified a connection between bats and dark forces by describing the devil's wings as being like those of a bat. This was further conveyed in early depictions of the devil and various demons with bat wings. Even today, demonic entities are still frequently shown with these features.

Given these associations, it's easy to see how there was a short jump that connected bats and witches. In some places, if bats were seen near a person or around an individual's house, it was thought to be an indication that they were in league with the devil. Case in point: in France in 1332, Lady Jacaume of Bayonne was accused of practicing witchcraft after bats were seen frequenting her garden. The woman was publicly burned to death because of her "crimes."

Bats and the Supernatural

On a broader scale, bats have long been associated with the supernatural. Their very nature—their nocturnal habits, erratic flying patterns and distinct shapes—have likely influenced this connection. At one time, people even believed that bats were miniature dragons.

Other world traditions consider the bat the guardian of the night who holds secrets that can only be found between the worlds. They are, after all, liminal creatures, an animal of the in-between. They come out at sunset as night is falling and just as the day is ending. They are a part of the natural order, but somehow just outside of it. On a physical level, they appear to be birds, and yet, they are mammals—the only mammals capable of true flight.

Native American beliefs about bats range widely from the Blackfoot who believed that bats were poisonous to tribes in the Pacific Northwest who believe bats are lucky animals.

In some cases, the bat plays the role of trickster in North America, though these tales are nowhere near as frequent as coyote trickster stories. Some Pueblo tribes of the American Southwest say that the movements of bats can predict the weather. According to the Navajo, bats can fly between the different worlds and act as a bridge between the natural and the supernatural. The Navajo also believed that bats represented hidden knowledge since they are able to navigate so easily in the dark.

In Tonga, people believed that bats were physical manifestations of the souls of the dead. According to traditions on the Ivory Coast, bats are the spirits of the dead.

Bats turn up a lot in South and Central American lore where they're frequently associated with the dead and the underworld. In parts of Mexico, it's believed that bats can carry messages from the dead.

In South America, among the ancient Mayan cult of the Quiche, there was a bat deity. Located in the jungles of what is now Guatemala, the god Camazotz was a minor deity associated with bats and the underworld. He was the god of caves and is described as having the body of a man and the head and wings of a bat.

The Mayan sacred book of initiation rituals, Popul Vuh, says that Camazotz lived in a bat house deep in the underworld amidst a maze of caves through which large bats flew. The deity was responsible for the seventh test of initiation given to the Mayan hero twins.

In the modern age, bats have become strongly associated with vampires—the dreaded undead nocturnal bloodsuckers. For the most part, this association comes from Dracula, the classic novel by Irish author Bram Stoker first published in 1897. Although the work was fictional, it did much to solidify bats in the supernatural spectrum and further heightened the fear of bats.

Stoker had a number of inspirations for his creation including the Wallachian prince Vlad Tepes, aka Vlad the Impaler, but the author may also have heard tales of South American vampire bats as well. The Spanish had come across vampire bats when they explored the Americas, so the stories were well-known, and likely exaggerated by the time they reached Europe.

Thousands of vampire stories, movies and television shows have further solidified the bat connection by associating bats as the companions of the undead. In many stories, human vampires have the ability to shapeshift into bat form for quick travel or escape.

Good Fortune

While the appearance of the bat has had a lot of fear attached to it in much of the western world, in China, the animal has long been viewed in a very different light. In China, if a bat flies into the home, it's a sign of good fortune for the family and people are happy to see the creatures come darting inside.

In Asia, bats are seen as a general sign of good luck and protection. They are frequently painted red to symbolize good fortune. Bats can also ward off diseases. This belief may have come about because of the fact that bats consume such a large number of insects including those that carry diseases.

In China, bats are a symbol of happiness and good fortune. An old Chinese custom is for mothers to sew bat-shaped jade buttons onto the clothing of babies to ensure that the child lives a long and happy life.

Vintage Asian tapestries, art and even Imperial robes often depict bats, usually in clusters of five. The five bats were said to be a five-fold blessing and represent: long life, prosperity, good health, a virtuous life, and a natural, peaceful death.

Myths & Facts

There are about 1,400 species of bats worldwide and they're found on every continent except Antarctica, so they're a common animal. For the most part, bats feed on insects and fruits, though some do prey on small rodents, and yes, there are actual vampire bats—three species of them, and they are found in Central and South America, but they are rather small in size.

There are some fascinating facts about bats. They eat an amazing number of insects—estimates indicate that a single bat can consume over 1,000 insects a night. In fact, if you have a mosquito problem in your neighborhood, putting out bat houses and attracting the nocturnal animals to your area can be very beneficial. According to data from the National Park Service, bats save humans 3.7 billion dollars a year in pest control. Bats also pollinate over 700 plants including peaches, bananas, mangoes and avocadoes, making them a vital component of the natural world.

On another level, bats are very social animals. They sleep in clusters, groom each other, and if a bat dies or is killed, other bats will take care of the orphaned young.

There are a number of common myths about bats that even today many people believe are true. The most common one is the idea that a bat can get stuck in a person's hair—stuck so thoroughly that the person's hair has to be cut off in order to get the animal loose.

This is a common myth that's often based on the idea that bats are blind (another myth). Most bats actually have very good eyesight which they use to navigate, search for food, and to avoid predators and other dangers. The myth that they are blind likely arose from their use of echolocation which they utilize at night. Echolocation gives bats the ability to "see" with both their eyes and ears.

I remember hearing the old wives tale about bats getting stuck in your hair when I was very young, but I never felt fearful of bats or the potential of one getting caught in my hair. Granted, they do seem to fly in very fast, erratic patterns, so perhaps this is what scares some people. In truth, bats have senses that are so sharp that they can detect a single strand of hair, so they certainly wouldn't fly directly into a mass of it.

The age-old fear of a bat stuck in one's hair led to several folkloric interpretations as to what it meant if this occurred. By many accounts, a bat stuck in your hair means that you will go mad. Another version says that if a bat gets stuck in someone's hair, that person will face eternal damnation. Neither one seems like a very good prospect.

The French have their own interpretation of this predicament. According to them, if someone gets a bat stuck in their hair it's symbolic that they will soon have a disastrous love affair. Leave it to the French to make it all about romance.

Bizarrely, in 1959, the Earl of Cranbrook decided to test the old story. Using a trio of female volunteers, the Earl tried to deliberately tangle bats in the hair of the three women. The Earl conducted his test using four different species of bat, but in each instance, the bats were able to escape the women's hair without any assistance. Thus, the Earl dispelled the odd superstition.

Another common myth is that all bats carry rabies. A study conducted by the University of Florida showed that less than one percent of bats carry the disease, so your chances of contracting rabies from a bat is incredibly slim.

Contrary to some common statements, bats are not rodents, nor are they even related to rodents. Bats belong to a separate class of animals known as *Chiroptera*, which translates as "hand-wing."

Yet another myth says that bat bites never heal. There is a very small thread of truth behind this one. When it comes to the bite of the vampire bat—the saliva of the vampire bat contains an anti-coagulant that stops blood from clotting while the animals are feeding. Scientists have been looking at this quality and its potential in modern medicine.

While people are now much more educated when it comes to bats, the influence of earlier superstitions and beliefs is still with us. Consider the use of bats in everyday language with various sayings such as "blind as a bat" for someone who can't see, or "bat out of hell" often used to describe someone driving in a fast or erratic manner. An old English phrase, "bats in the belfry," was once used to describe someone who was a bit insane and the modern "Batty" is a version of this. For someone who's acting really off balance there's the more adult "bat s**t crazy."

As always, it's not entirely bad news with bats though. One of the world's most popular and well-known superheroes, Batman, took his inspiration from the nocturnal creatures. Bruce Wayne, the man who became Batman, was inspired to create his famous alter ego when a bat flew through the window and into Wayne Manor, leading Bruce to adopt the guise of a creature that could strike fear into the hearts of criminals. Apparently, a bat in the house wasn't bad news for Bruce.

Resources and Works Consulted:

Allen, Glover Morrill. *Bats: Biology, Behavior and Folklore*. Dover Publications, 2004.

Frembgen, Jurgen Wasim. "Embodying Evil and Bad Luck: Stray Notes on the Folklore of Bats in Southwest Asia." *Asian Folklore Studies*, Volume 65, Issue 2, 2006.

Kunz, Thomas H. "Halloween Treat: Bat Facts and Folklore." *The American Biology Teacher*, 6:7. 1984.

McCracken, Gary F. "Bats in Belfries and Other Places. *BATS Magazine*, Volume 10, Issue 4, 1992.

McCracken, Gary F. "Folklore and the Origin of Bats." *BATS Magazine*. Volume 11, Issue 4, 1993.

National Park Service website "Benefits of Bats."

Storm, Caleb. "Batman Existed in Mesoamerican Mythology and His Name was Camazotz." *Ancient Origins* online magazine, 2019.

The Dead Have Company: Monsters in Midwest Graveyards

By: Chad Lewis

Long ago when your loved one passed away, you would lovingly bury them in the family resting ground. Typically, these small family plots were located in a tucked away piece of earth somewhere on your property. Once the majority of burials moved away from family farms to larger public graveyards, the location of where the cemeteries should be placed became an important decision. Plots of available land were chosen in part due to the fact that they represented a portal between our world and the spirit world---making it easier for your loved one to travel from our world to whatever world you believe they go to. If possible, graveyards were placed on the other side of rivers and lakes due to the old belief that ghosts, monsters, and other supernatural beings could not pass over running water—thus the water acted as a supernatural moat between the town and burial ground. Even with these precautions, mourners would take numerous separate winding paths back to town to ensure that vengeful spirits would not be able to follow them home. If you were truly afraid that someone you had wronged in life would come back from the grave to seek revenge, you might even paint your house a different color in hopes that the spirit will not recognize it as your home and will terrorize your neighbors instead. Yet regardless of the rituals and procedures that were implemented to thwart this, the graveyard itself remained as a place where all sorts of supernatural beings lurked.

Years ago, cemeteries were much more multi-functional than they are today. Back then, cemeteries were thought of as public spaces that were often used for family reunions and daily picnics. Heck, people even camped and slept in graveyards. Today, however, our cemeteries are mostly seen as just memorials for our deceased. This decrease of usage seems to have produced unforeseen outcomes because when the general public thinks of haunted places, they often think of graveyards. Largely overshadowed by ghostly legends and lore, graveyards are chock full of all manner of mysterious creatures that are far more bizarre than you could ever imagine.

Monkey Wolf

Take notice of the fact that the Monkey Wolf headline is not plural, because as far as I know, the Monkey Wolf you are about to be introduced to is the only known legend of its kind. Perhaps this is a good thing, because legend tells that this odd creature roams a cemetery that might just take your life.

Witches

Believe it or not, witches are one of the most reported monsters to dwell in the darkness of graveyards. Often said to be vindictive and seeking revenge at those who took their lives years, decades, or even centuries ago, they tend to act as the graveyard protectors who are quick to curse anyone who is foolish enough to go searching for them.

Lake Monsters/ Sea Serpents

As previously mentioned, water played an important role in the choosing of where to put graveyards. With so many cemeteries sharing borders with lakes, rivers, and streams, it is no wonder that creatures of the water sometimes slink their way onto land as well. While by no means as prevalent as the other hideous monsters profiled here, lake monsters like to occasionally mingle with the dead.

Hellhounds

Throughout history, cultures from around the world have told of large black dogs with glowing red eyes patrolling sacred areas, burial grounds and even alleged portals to Hell. Their association with the Devil is a widespread belief as they are often thought to do Old Scratch's bidding and have traditionally been seen as omens of death. It is not difficult to see why hellhounds have been tied to graveyards because in many old beliefs and superstitions the spirit of the first burial at a cemetery would be responsible for watching over and forever protecting the graveyard. Not wanting to curse any human with this eternal task, people would often kill a black dog and bury it in the far northern most corner of the cemetery where it would serve as a supernatural watch dog for the deceased.

Vampires

Out of all supernatural beings, perhaps none are as closely associated with graveyards as Vampires. Throughout history these undead beings have been believed to literally live in the cemetery. Whether it is in a decrepit mausoleum, musty dilapidated coffin, or simply in a hollowed-out hole in the ground surrounded by the earth of their homeland, these sinister beings of the dark are the embodiment of death. Even though they freely drift from cemetery grounds in search of prey, they will invariably return to their home.

Werewolves

Typically reported to be large bipedal beasts with long muzzles, thick matted down fur, razor sharp claws, and long deadly teeth, werewolves have strangely been spotted in and around places of burial. The reason for this fondness of graveyards is unknown; perhaps it is the seclusion of many of these cemeteries, or maybe the fresh scent of death or rotting flesh is irresistible to them. Regardless of the reason, many cemeteries add werewolves to their list of occupants.

The Monkey Wolf

I put the case of the monkey wolf first among all these otherworldly creatures because it may be my absolute favorite graveyard creature. It makes it even more fascinating because I have never heard of another similar type of creature. Yet as spectacular as the monkey wolf may be, it is by no means the star of this cemetery. In fact, hardly anyone knows of this creature at all. I have found that some of the best legends and folklore come directly from those hidden pockets of America where outside of a few residents of the area, the legend remains largely unknown. Without a doubt, when most people hear about Riverside Cemetery in Marshalltown, Iowa, they will undoubtedly think about the cursed Death Chair that rests in the cemetery.

The legend involving the death chair of Riverside Cemetery is amazingly simple –DO NOT sit in the chair! The legend tells that anyone who is foolish enough to stand on, sit in, or merely touch the chair will suffer great misfortune and die. One popular variation of the dare claims that if you sit in the chair at midnight, you will die within one year. Or it is even better if you sit in the chair at midnight on your birthday or on Halloween! Other variations run the gamut in terms of what consequences will befall you after you complete the dare: all types of car accidents, mishaps, misfortune, and an untimely death.

As I previously mentioned, the death chair is not the cemetery's only source of supernatural notoriety. Just down the path from the death chair resides an old receiving vault that had been turned into a private mausoleum. According to legend, a man buried his wife in this mausoleum; the only weird part was that his wife was alive when he buried her. Now many unsuspecting cemetery visitors have reported hearing odd noises coming from inside the crypt, including a woman's voice crying out for help, saying things like "Help me I can't breathe," "Let me out," "Don't leave me in here." There have also been frequent reports of people hearing mysterious rapping and banging from the inside of the crypt. Others swear that they have seen the mausoleum's locked door handle jiggle and move on its own.

Over the course of my research into the paranormal, I have heard countless legends involving all sorts of weird creatures: every shape, size, and color you can imagine. From corpse eating ghoul snakes to vanishing phantom chickens,

I thought I had heard it all. Luckily, I hadn't, as evidenced by the 2017 conversation I had with a woman who told me that her uncle and father had always talked about some sort of monkey wolf inhabiting the old cemetery. Apparently appearing as though it was part monkey and part wolf, the creature was thought to live in the forested area at the back of the graveyard. It should be noted that the back of the cemetery juts up against a sloped forest and wooded area providing much needed cover and habitat for anything looking to not be discovered.

The origin of the monkey wolf is virtually unknown, as the woman who told me about it had no idea where her family had first heard of the beast. I have visited the cemetery on many occasions, and have presented at numerous libraries throughout the region and I have yet to encounter anyone who is familiar with the monkey wolf of Riverside Cemetery. Unfortunately, the woman I spoke with was unable to recall any further details regarding this amazing legend and the physical makeup of this beast is left to your imagination. My hope is that in the future, as more people become aware of the legend, they will keep an eye out for the monkey wolf and additional sightings will surface.

The Hellhounds of 13 Step Cemetery

If you are trying to locate 13 Step Cemetery, do NOT ask the locals of Palo, Iowa, for directions. Due to a never-ending parade of curious legend trippers, and some unfortunate graveyard vandalism, locals will purposely direct you away from the cemetery, or even feign ignorance about knowing anything about the local cemetery. Those of a more optimistic outlook would contend that the townsfolk are not being rude, but rather doing their due diligence in keeping you alive.

To say that 13 Step Cemetery is isolated would be an understatement. This is one of those cemeteries you don't merely bump into. Unless you are actively searching for it, you would have a difficult time locating it. However, for those persistent enough to find it will be treated to a smorgasbord of paranormal happenings.

From the minute you park your car in the makeshift gravel lot, the weirdness is already upon you—you just don't realize it yet. I will get to that a little later, but for now, the best way to enter the cemetery is by ascending the old crumbling concrete stairs that sit in front of the graveyard like a demented gatekeeper daring you to enter. If you visit the cemetery in the daytime, there will be 12 steps leading up to the graves, However, if you are foolish enough to venture out in the night, a mysterious 13th step will appear and guide you into the cursed graveyard---hence the name 13 Step Cemetery. It is certainly not a coincidence that the number of steps changes from 12 to the number 13---as many believe that it is precisely the bad luck that comes with the number 13 that will accompany you through the graveyard.

At this point in the cemetery, people begin to hear strange voices echoing through the wooded area that envelops the cemetery like a snug winter coat, although the likelihood of another human presence is slim. Disembodied lights often float through the area, changing in size, shape, and color, as they travel from grave to grave. It is important that with all this weird activity taking place you keep an eye out because the cemetery is also thought to be the home of huge black hellhounds that are said to protect the cemetery from unwanted visitors.

Most who are lucky (or unfortunate) enough to see these hellhounds are only able to see the faint outline of them as they patrol the perimeter of the graveyard. Others have a more close-up encounter. A few years back I spoke with a group of paranormal researchers who ventured out to the cemetery one night to put all the legends to the test. As they were walking around getting the lay of the land, a giant phantom black dog darted right past them as they stood frozen with fear. Due to the humongous size of the creature, they were convinced that the passing beast was not some stray black dog from a nearby farm.

Strangely, all of the weird activity is not confined to the cemetery proper. As I mentioned earlier, strange things happen when in the parking area as well. On numerous occasions visitors to the secluded cemetery walk back to their cars only to find that someone or something has placed dead animals on their hood. Reports of bloody raccoons and other small game animals discarded on cars only enhances the fears that the graveyard Hellhounds are all too real.

The Mineral Point Vampire

I spent some time roaming through the rural countryside of Transylvania searching for strange legends and folklore about vampires. Little did I know, if I wanted to find vampires, I should have stayed in my home state of Wisconsin. Well, Mineral Point, Wisconsin, to be exact.

Mineral Point is a small rural community tucked into the rolling hills of southwest Wisconsin. The quiet, charming little community is overflowing with history. Although the origins of the town date back to 1827-1828, it wouldn't be until much later that the town made international headlines for being the home to numerous vampire sightings.

Mineral Point's official Vampire troubles began back on Monday, March 30, 1981, when Officer Jon Pepper was out on night patrol. The *Lexington Herald* reported, "Pepper was routinely shining his light through Graceland Cemetery when he saw 'a huge person with a white-painted face' wearing a dark cape." Officer Pepper quickly exited the car and chased the Dracula-looking creature across the sacred earth, but he finally gave up when the lightning-fast creature somehow disappeared among the gravestones and flew over a cemetery fence. Although it was in the dead of night, Officer Pepper was able to catch a decent glimpse of the thing as it raced through the graveyard. Pepper described the cloaked figure as being over 6 feet 3 inches in height, pale, thin, and very ugly. Pepper's weird description of the creature only served to make the case even more bizarre.

Back at his car, Officer Pepper tried to calm himself down from the unsuccessful capture of the trespasser. He was hesitant to make his report, as he knew how outlandish the story would sound. Regardless of the consequences, Pepper was on duty and felt that it was his sworn duty to file the report. Once Officer Pepper's report got out, media from all over the country descended upon the small town, looking for the Mineral Point Vampire. The publicity from the report generated a full-fledged vampire frenzy in town. Within hours of the news reports, dozens of additional sightings of the mysterious vampire poured in to the authorities, causing the *Wisconsin State Journal* to run the story "Vampires Stalk Mineral Point." The newspaper quoted Lt. Bill Trott as saying, "Last night (Tuesday) we had a half-dozen vampires on the loose in town." Lt. Trott continued his report, "We received several phone calls and were stopped by people on the street reporting encounters with white-faced creepy-looking people jumping out of the shadows at them." All of these separate accounts led to the theory that these sightings were not simply the work of one lone person or creature. Not surprisingly, the official police explanation had little to do with vampires, as they believed that the rash of subsequent sightings were the work of pranksters who took advantage of Officer Pepper's sighting and decided to cause some mischief of their own.

The police also proposed a more mundane explanation for Officer Pepper's sighting, theorizing that the mysterious intruder of the cemetery was not in fact a vampire, but was instead someone suffering from a mental illness. Perhaps, this explained the police department's hesitation to pursue the case further as the *Anderson Independent*, picking up on the story, reported that the police were not eager to get back to the cemetery. "'I can't get anyone to go back to the cemetery at night,' Lt. William Trott said. 'I even offered to pay Pepper overtime to stake out the place for his vampire, but he wouldn't bite,' added the lawman with a chuckle." The unique phrasing chosen by Lt. Trott including "stake and bite" makes me wonder if he was having a bit of fun at the expense of the press. Even if Lt. Trott was being playful with the semantics of the story, the *Wisconsin State Journal* reported that "Trott swears his report is not an April Fool's Joke."

For years I tried to track down Officer Pepper to get his take on the whole situation. Local legends state that Officer Pepper was so plagued by all the unwanted attention his story had garnered that he quit the police force, moved away, and refused to speak of the event ever again. It seems he doesn't want to revisit the case, as my many requests for an interview or comment have gone unanswered or maybe they have disappeared into the night…just like the Vampire of 1981.

When I first began researching this case, I had a very telling and perplexing experience. I began by visiting the local law enforcement office. When I asked the front desk clerk about the legend, she informed me that the entire thing was completely made up and the incident/report of officer Pepper never actually happened. I found this to be a strange, if not deceitful answer since I was holding a newspaper photo of officer Pepper standing in the cemetery talking to reporters about his sightings. When I showed the desk clerk this newspaper photo, she told me to "wait here while I get my supervisor." A few minutes later the supervisor showed up and politely informed me that yes, there actually was a report filed by officer Pepper, but unfortunately all of those files were destroyed in a fire a few years back. Was this another bout of subterfuge by the police department looking to cover-up a strange vampire sighting? I am not sure how to answer that question. To this day, many people still believe that there is a strange immortal vampire lurking in Graceland Cemetery. However, I can tell you the best way to find out if a vampire creature is roaming Graceland Cemetery is by visiting the graveyard for yourself---just don't forget to bring a vampire hunting kit.

The Fowler Lake Monster

Along the shoreline of Oconomowoc, Wisconsin's Lake Fowler rests the haunted La Belle Cemetery. In fact, the sea serpent legend of the lake takes a back seat to the infamous stories of the supernatural activity that is said to plague the graveyard. However, even though the majority of curious legend trippers visiting the cemetery might be unaware of a lake monster lurking in the water, the haunted legend itself ensures that the monster legend will not be ignored. Here is what I mean by that.

Outside of the giant beast, Fowler Lake has another remarkable connection to the supernatural that comes in the form of some haunted statuary. Visitors to the suburban looking cemetery report encounters of disembodied lights and mysterious noises, but the overwhelming majority of people who visit the cemetery come to see the moving statue.

Legend tells of a young woman who went swimming out in Fowler Lake, only to tire out quickly. With no one around to help her, the lake became her watery grave. After the tragedy, her bloated body was buried in a proper grave next to the very lake that took her life. A giant statue was placed atop the woman's grave. Legend states that if you visit the woman's grave at night (of course), several anomalies can be witnessed. The statue's hands will turn black right in front of you, and blood will ooze out of its eyes. Yet, the most bizarre legend tells of the statue actually coming to life and recreating the woman's drowning in the lake. Those who have seen her move claim that as soon as the statue descends into Fowler Lake, it instantaneously returns to its grave. Perhaps even the ghostly statue of a drowned woman is frightened by what lurks in Fowler Lake.

In 1876, a letter written by a Wisconsin resident found its way to the *Chicago Tribune*. The letter provided, in great detail, several of the large "fish" stories of Fowler Lake. The writer told the tale of "old Lop-Jaw," a notoriously elusive fish whose uncanny ability to escape capture was only equaled by its gargantuan size. The prized catch became something of an obsession for a Dr. Henshall, who claimed that the beast was "as long as an oar." The doctor was lucky enough to actually hook the monster before it easily shook its head and spit out the lure, which shot up twenty feet into the air. Judging by the strength with which the beast tugged on his pole, the doctor believed the beast must have easily weighed over 100 pounds. Distinguishing "old Lop-Jaw" from other fish in the lake was pretty simple due to the fact that it was missing one half of its face, and the other half was pierced with numerous hanging lures. Knowing that its favorite hangouts were down by the dam, Church Point, and the bay at Draper's Hall, also increased the chances of finding it.

An 1892 *Chicago Tribune* article touting Wisconsin's lake monsters spent most of its space on the legend of Fowler Lake. In June of 1886, Mr. C.I. Peck was fishing on the lake when "a very large object" caught his notice, and prompted him to steer his boat toward the object. As he inched his way forward, the unknown beast appeared to be a fish and, judging by the portion that was visible, the thing was huge. Peck estimated that the beast was no smaller than eight feet in length and had to weigh upwards of sixty or seventy pounds. If we can believe Mr. Peck's estimates, both the length and weight of the beast would be far too great to be attributed to any known fish in the lake.

In the summer of 1905, Fowler Lake was once again abuzz with talks of a giant fish—this time it was thought to be a huge pickerel. The *Waukesha Freeman* recounted the intriguing story of a Mr. Griffith, who had rigged up a "specially strong spoon" in hopes of landing the new prized fish, which was estimated to be around forty pounds. Luckily, Griffith was able to hook the monster, and furiously fought with it for over a half hour in hopes of tiring it out. Finally, another fisherman, Tom Francey, grabbed a net and came to Griffith's aid just as the line snapped, and the fish darted off, with the special lure hanging out of its mouth.

Today, the ghost of the young woman who met her fate in the lake is said to lure curious visitors to the banks of the water to witness her spirit reenacting her death, or perhaps to get a closer look at the lake monster as well.

The Terrifying Witch of Pere Cheney

Far from the beaten path, hidden on the overgrown outskirts of the long-forgotten ghost town of Pere Cheney, Michigan, lies the old Pere Cheney Cemetery. You won't find the village of Pere Cheney on any modern maps, and if you rely solely on your GPS to take you there, you will be out of luck as well. For all intents and purposes, the town of Pere Cheney no longer exists.

Once known for its bright future and the endless possibilities for its residents, today the ghost town is best known for a wild witch who roams the ground, keeping all the active spirits company. This place provides an interesting contradiction. Normally when a town has been gone for nearly a century, people tend to forget that it even existed. Yet, when I traveled to the area to investigate this case, I discovered that the town of Pere Cheney was well-known to nearly everyone I spoke with. At first glance, this doesn't seem to make any sort of sense, but when you factor in the legend that the area is cursed with death and heartache, the fascination of keeping Pere Cheney alive becomes crystal clear. So how does an abandoned and forgotten town become widely known as a place for ghosts and witches? That answer is easy—misery, suffering, tragedy, and death!

The main legend told to me by person after person went like this. In the early days the town was buzzing with people and commerce alike. But as fate would have it, prosperity was not in the cards for the new town, and during the 1880s the village was ravaged by diphtheria. In order to stop the spread of the infectious disease, and spare additional families from death, the townspeople took the drastic measure of burning down what remained of their town. Being the hearty folk that they were, the town was soon rebuilt and residents began to carry on with their everyday lives. Just as things were returning to some semblance of normal, a second deadly wave of disease ripped through the village, wiping out scores of people. Superstitious folks began worrying that perhaps the town was cursed and that people ought to leave the town while they still could. By the early 1900s, the town was completely abandoned, inhabited only by the souls of those who met their end in Pere Cheney.

The combination of death, disease, and cursed land come together to make a wonderfully intriguing and gruesome story, but is the tantalizing legend accurate? After digging through the old newspaper accounts, talking with the regional historical society, and speaking with local residents, I have pieced together how the story really unfolded…and unfortunately it still remains just as dark and tragic as the legend says.

In 1883, the town was ravaged by a bout of diphtheria that took the lives of many local children. Ten years later, in 1893, the town was once again struck with smallpox, scarlet fever, and diphtheria, resulting in another large round of deaths, many of which can be verified by the cemetery gravestones. Believe it or not, in 1906, diphtheria once again punished the town with death and misery. With three major outbreaks in such a limited span of time, it is easy to see why people might have considered the town to be cursed. By 1914, the town of Pere Cheney was all but abandoned. However, I was unable to find any evidence that the town was burned down in protest to fate. It seems much more plausible that residents simply got siphoned away to the larger cities of Grayling and Roscommon in search of economic opportunities.

> not, the area has a bad past. Once the vibrant county seat, a Detroit Free Press article from 1878 described it as "a thriving farming community where one might 'breathe the purest atmosphere this side of the Rocky Mountains.' "
>
> It boasted 1,500 residents, three saw mills, a doctor, a school, and other amenities. What happened is unclear, but the legend is that the "witch" cursed the town. In those days, witches had less to do with a role as a spell caster and more with her responsibility as a single mom who was banished from a life among the more righteous townsfolk. Her child died, and she went mad and cursed the town's children.
>
> ***Detroit Free Press***, *May 7, 2017*

No one is quite sure as to the origin of the cemetery's paranormal reputation. Many seniors of the area that I spoke with recalled hearing stories of weird events occurring while they were youngsters. For decades the cemetery was left desecrated and in a state of continual disrepair. Weeds and tall grass had overtaken the once manicured grounds, vandals had ruthlessly busted up and kicked over gravestones, and trash was strewn about the place as if it were a county dump.

The total seclusion of the cemetery tends to attract many teenagers who go there to party away from the watchful eye of their parents or the police. Legend tells of many visitors who unwisely decided to take a piece of the cemetery home with them only to discover that bad luck seemed to dwell all around them. It happened so many times that teenagers began daring one another to take something from the graveyard, and with that the dare of Pere Cheney was born. For many years, the cemetery caretakers have battled against persistent vandalism, so my advice is that if you really want to take something from the graveyard, make sure it is a piece of trash or garbage. Remember that the curse is only broken when you return the item. Luckily for me, the old graveyard had plenty of recently discarded items for me to pick from. I chose an old beer can that I still have not returned. Perhaps I should heed the advice of those witnesses I interviewed because I spoke with a group of friends that had driven out to the cemetery to camp and party the night away. It was a long night and numerous beers had been consumed, and a lot of cans had been discarded throughout the cemetery by the time the group finally drifted off to seep. When the blazing sun finally woke the sleeping teens, they noticed that all the beer cans had been picked up and thrown neatly into the garbage can. They believed that the spirits had cleaned up the cemetery while they slept.

Teenagers are not the only ones drawn to the cemetery, as I spoke with a local man in his 40s who would often walk out to the cemetery to check out all of the old grave markers. He said that every time he walked through the cemetery, he would get the odd sense that he was not alone; he felt as though some unseen presence was watching his every move. On several occasions, these odd feelings would occur just before he saw several strange figures moving throughout the cemetery. The man never did find out who or what the figures were. One of the most popular legends of the cemetery involves a woman that once lived in Pere Cheney. Apparently, townsfolk believed that the woman was a witch, so they dragged her from town out to the cemetery where she was hanged and burned on a tree, forever trapping her spirit in the cemetery. Although I found no actual accounts of any "witch" or non-witch being hanged and burned in the cemetery, I did coincidently speak with several witnesses who told similar stories of seeing the ghostly image of a woman hanging from one of the cemetery trees. Others tells stories of being chased out of the graveyard by the screeching witch.

Be warned, though, this cemetery is exceptionally hard to get to. Even with detailed directions, I found myself turned around more times than I cared to count. After several hours of frustrated maneuvering, I finally found an access point leading to the cemetery, yet the lone road was so gutted with treacherous grooves and deep potholes, it became impassable. Exiting the car, I had no choice but to walk the final portion of roadway. With my first step into the cemetery, I could immediately see why the place had taken on such a haunted reputation. With broken and scattered gravestones, overgrown vegetation, and an overall uneasy feeling to it, the cemetery looked like something straight out of a horror movie. After reading over many of the diphtheria victims' gravestones, it became quite clear this horror movie was all too real. Knowing that many of those buried in the cemetery met a horrible end only enhanced the sadness that seemed to seep directly from the gravesites. I once saw a play where the premise was that you remained in Heaven only as long as there was someone living that remembered you. As I strolled through the grounds I couldn't help but wonder if the witch haunting this old cemetery was merely trying to keep the memory of Pere Cheney alive just a little bit longer.

The Werewolf of Ramsey Cemetery

When we think of creatures inhabiting caves, werewolves are usually not the first thing that spring to mind. Dark, damp caves seem like the perfect habitat for legends of trolls, Bigfoot, or giant bat-like flying humanoids like the Van Meter Visitor or Mothman. The prevailing belief about werewolves is that they are shape-shifters, so why would they hunker down in a musty cold cave when they can just transform back into human form and relax in the comfort of their own home? The key point to make here is that it seems that werewolves are not using the dark shallow caves surrounding Effingham Iowa's Ramsey Cemetery to live in, they are using it to ambush their prey!

Although tales of the area's supernatural activity have been percolating throughout the region for decades, the old cemetery continues to remain hidden deep in the thick woods, practically cloaked by Mother Nature's trees, farmland, and foreboding caves. But be warned, the beautiful landscape may give you the false sense of being completely alone...which is true, if you don't count ghosts and werewolves.

I was a bit surprised at just how far back the weird legends of the area extend. In 2006, I spoke with two senior women who told me that when they were kids during the 1940s, mischievous boys would often try to lure them out to the caves in order to really scare them. Although this is as far back as I was able to track the legend, the cemetery was established in 1851, so I have to wonder how many odd stories predate the 1940s. If you have read any of my previous writings on the subject of fear, dating, and the supernatural, you will know that experiencing fear with someone is a surefire way to bond with them. For generations smitten teens have tried to scare one another in hopes of becoming romantically closer to them, never knowing they were simply following the science of fear.

Several sources I spoke with told me about a gruesome suicide that occurred in the cemetery. Years ago, there was an old chapel in the cemetery that was used mainly for funerals and ceremonies. One dark evening in the 1960s a distraught young man drove out to the chapel. Once there, he grabbed a gun from the trunk of his car, walked inside the chapel, and blew his head off. In another version of the same legend, the young man chose hanging as his preferred method of death. The next day his lifeless body was found dangling from the end of a rope. Although the first legend is close to the truth, here is how the story actually went. On March 14, 1961, the dead body of a 39-year-old man was discovered in the cemetery's chapel. Newspaper reports claimed that the man had died of an apparent self-inflicted gun-shot wound. Soon after the horrible suicide, people began whispering about the chapel being haunted. The legend told that if you went inside the chapel, you would see blood oozing from the walls. Apparently, the macabre legend attracted so many curious visitors that officials eventually had to tear down the chapel due in part to all the vandalism that occurred. Unfortunately, I have been unable to find an exact date of the chapel's demolition.

Many curious visitors prefer to travel to the cemetery at night. A local woman told me that during summer evenings she used to go to the cemetery with a group of friends and watch for the ghosts that were said to roam the cemetery and caves.

Years ago, I also spoke with the cemetery sexton who is responsible for the maintenance and upkeep of the graveyard. Through the years, he had heard endless stories of people encountering spirits while visiting the cemetery. While on the job, he had personally encountered many weird things. On one occasion, he was walking toward the back of the cemetery when he stumbled upon a gruesome discovery. Pinned up on one of the old trees was the bloody dismembered body of a crucified possum. In addition to the desecrated possum, the sexton has routinely found strange symbols and bizarre offerings hanging from the cemetery trees. Although these types of discoveries would normally point to the occult, knowing that there are sightings of werewolves in and around the cemetery adds a bit more intensity to finding ripped apart animals.

My favorite part of Ramsey Cemetery is that in order to get to the cemetery, you have to travel down a pot-holed dirt road that is narrowly cut through the woods. It is on the side of this road that a series of caves are cut away into the landscape. Many of those I spoke with had heard tales of people encountering a large hairy monster that inhabits the caves.

Witnesses say the creature is tall, covered in thick matted-down hair, has a long muzzle, and is equipped with razor sharp claws and long fangs. By all accounts, the monster is a werewolf. The creepy creature is said to use the caves as its lair, a hidden place where it can safely store the remains of its human prey. Others have spotted glowing red eyes emanating from the caves. The red glare can be seen blazing through the dark night.

Those of you who are not too eager to come face to face with a werewolf can still get in on the action. The good news is that whatever this werewolf-looking creature truly is, its main focus seems to be self-preservation. In an effort to remain hidden and undiscovered, whenever the monster is spotted it tends to scurry back to the caves rather than attack. The monster is more prone to attack when it can sneak up on the unsuspecting victim. Either way, when you go searching for the werewolf, you best hope you spot IT before it sees YOU!

The Witches of Loon Lake Cemetery

The first thing you will notice upon entering Loon Lake Cemetery is a yellow printed paper sign claiming "No Ghosts or Witches exist in Loon Lake Cemetery." However, you don't have to take their word for it, you don't have to take my word for it, you can visit the rural cemetery and decide for yourself whether vengeful witches are roaming about.

If there is ever a place that looks like it should be inhabited by witches, Jackon, Minnesota's Loon Lake Cemetery is it. It has all the Hollywood trademarks of a haunted cemetery, with the eeriness of the area beginning right as you make your way through the small county-run park and begin to notice the seclusion of the area starting to creep in. If anything goes wrong, you best be prepared…because help would not arrive for quite some time. As you meander along the overgrown make-shift trail that leads up to the cemetery, the mixture of the isolation and the apparent lack of any cemetery caretaker all but dares you to discover the graves of the witches. If you make it out to the overgrown cemetery, you have completed the easy portion of the adventure.

There are so many versions of the Loon Lake Cemetery legend that the actual truth has all but been forgotten by those simply looking to scare themselves with a creepy tale of witchcraft, murder, and revenge. To help simplify the legends, I will try to sort the facts from fiction.

The most well-known and ominous of the legends tells of a young woman named Mary Jane Twiliger (Twillegar, Twiliger, Terwilleger, etc…), who was rumored to be involved in the practice of witchcraft. Being that it was the 1800s, the overly superstitious among the community did not look kindly on Mary's devilish rituals and set out to put an end to them—which they did by chopping off Mary's head with an ax. Mary's gruesome body, along with the bloody ax, was buried in Loon Lake cemetery. With her burial, the townsfolk believed that it was the end of the story. However, as they would soon find out, the story was just beginning. Shortly after Mary's death, residents began to whisper about strange happenings out at the cemetery, which were immediately attributed to Mary's vengeful spirit. A few short years later, Clarinda Allen, another suspected young witch, was also decapitated and buried out at the cemetery. The town must have been plagued with witches, because legend tells of a third young woman who met her fate at the hands of the frightened and murderous community. Unfortunately, the third woman's name has been lost to history. The Loon Lake Cemetery was quickly filling up with suspected witches, which gave rise to the stories of the place being cursed. Over the years, the legends grew to monstrous proportions…eventually leading to the tale that anyone who is foolish enough to jump over the graves of the murdered witches would suffer tremendous bouts of bad luck and may even die due to their unwise decisions.

It is an amazing legend, but is any of it actually true? The answer to that question is a bit trickier than a simple yes or no. First of all, it looks as though 17-year-old Mary Terwilliger was not beheaded at all. According to the March 18, 1880, edition of the *Spirit Lake Beacon*, Mary met death at the hands of the more mundane manner of diphtheria while living in Cherokee County, Iowa. Mary's body was originally buried in Spirit Lake until her family moved to Minnesota and decided to reinter Mary's body at the Loon Lake Cemetery. As for the other two alleged witches, no known evidence has been found to either dismiss or substantiate the claims.

Regardless of the real history behind Mary Jane, visitors to the cemetery reported all manner of paranormal activity. Tales of floating balls of lights floating through the area, mysterious apparitions, disembodied voices echoing through the graves. Eventually visitors started taking the dare which told that if you were brave enough (or foolish enough) to jump over, walk past, or merely touch a witches' grave, you would be cursed with bad luck until the day you die.

For years, I had collected stories of people visiting the witch's grave only to report tales of mishaps, misfortune, and death. Everything from accidents and work firings to speeding tickets and death have been blamed on the cemetery. After one of my presentations, a young woman approached me and asked if I knew of any way to break the Loon Lake curse.

Apparently, she had gone out to the cemetery late at night with a group of friends. One of her brother's friends, looking to show off his bravery to the captive audience, decided to jump over as many gravesites as he could while mocking the legend the entire time. As the night progressed, the group began to get bored since nothing out of the ordinary was happening and returned home disappointed. The next day, the young woman was awoken by her phone ringing. On the other end was her brother. He informed her that after dropping everybody off, the daring grave-jumping young man was involved in a serious car accident that placed him in the hospital.

I had heard so many stories that when I first visited the cemetery for myself, I was excited to take the dare for myself. The only problem is that no one knows which grave(s) holds the witch. Many of the graves are unmarked; even the old plat books do not accurately tell who is buried where. Mary Jane, the alleged witch, well, her gravestone was removed from the cemetery and placed in the safety of the Jackson County Historical Society, due to fears that it would be stolen by some overzealous legend tripper.

One of the more interesting and creepy aspects of the cemetery is the ability of visitors to spend the night in the nearby self-registering campground—which sits right outside of the path leading to the graveyard. For those who have done so, they often report hearing the faint wailing of a female voice drifting out from the area of the cemetery. One such camper contacted me after spending a nearly sleepless night sitting up inside his tent while trying to figure out where the womanly cries were coming from. Believing that a relaxing camping trip was actually what he needed to de-stress from a hectic work week, the young man departed for the campground. While setting up his tent, he marveled at the peacefulness of the area. Little did he know that the atmosphere was about to take a turn for the worse. Tucked inside his two-person tent, the young man eased back and enjoyed the quiet as he prepared for a good night's sleep. Trying to keep his mind from thoughts of work, the quiet was broken by the sound of a woman talking in a voice so slight that he was unable to make out what she was saying. Unzipping his tent, he stuck out his head hoping to see a fellow camper passing by. Only the stars in the sky were outside as the man popped back into the tent and quickly settled in. Just before dozing off, the voice returned…this time it was a bit louder, but it still remained unintelligible.

Convinced that someone was trying to scare him or playing a trick, he grabbed his flashlight and headed out to investigate. Again, the frustrated man found the area completely empty. Now a pattern was starting to emerge whereby every time he was closing in on sleep, the female voice would interrupt, forcing him to sit up and listen. This bizarre ritual was repeated several more times, and each time the man would sit up and listen intently for the source of the voice, which never came. Finally, morning arrived and the drowsy young man packed up and prepared to leave. On his way out he stopped in at the office to ask if anyone else had reported anything similar that evening. The man stated that the voice sounded as though it were coming from the area by the hill, only to discover that the area of the voice was exactly where the cemetery was. Since we truly do not know where the witch(es) are buried, my advice is that you avoid every gravestone you see, thereby decreasing the chances that the witch will come after you.

As you can see from all of these bizarre creatures, cemeteries are no longer just the domain of the dead, they are the fertile hunting, breeding, and living quarters for all sorts of unspeakable monstrosities. Today, more and more people than ever before are choosing to be cremated, which means that we will have whole generations of people who do not have any recent relatives buried in a cemetery---thus propelling a large decrease in the number of people who visit a graveyard. This decrease will only make graveyards more isolated and desolate, which is probably exactly what all the various mysterious creatures that call cemeteries home would prefer!

Resources and Works Consulted:

Anderson Independent. April 3, 1981.

Chicago Tribune. July 24, 1892.

Daily Democrat. September 3, 1889.

Lewis, Chad. *The Minnesota Road Guide to Mysterious Creatures*. On the Road Publications. 2011.

Lewis, Chad. *Supernatural Dares of the Midwest: Curses, Monsters, and Ghosts*. On the Road Publications. 2021.

Lewis, Chad & Fisk, Terry. *The Iowa Road Guide to Haunted Locations*. Unexplained Publishing. 2007.

Lexington Herald. April 3, 1981.

Logansport Journal. September 3,1889.

Spirit Lake Beacon, March 18, 1880.

Waukesha Freeman. August 18, 1892.

Wisconsin State Journal. April 2, 1981.

Beware the Melonheads!

By David Weatherly

Imagine being on a lonely backroad on the outskirts of town. It's late at night and you're all alone. You see something dart quickly across the road. At first, you're thinking perhaps it was a coyote or deer, but it looked almost…human. A moment later, you round a bend on the old lane and there it is, standing in the middle of the road illuminated in your high beams. A person…sort of… dressed in rags, about three feet tall with spindly arms and a very large, strangely shaped head.

You've just encountered a melonhead!

Melonhead legends can be found in numerous places including Ohio and Michigan, but they seem to be especially prominent in the state of Connecticut where several towns have melonhead tales. For the sake of brevity, this article will focus on the Nutmeg State and its legends about the big-headed beings.

As the name suggests, the melonheads have large, bulbous, bald heads. They also have big, bulging red eyes, crooked teeth, long skinny arms and short torsos. They're usually described as being short—about three feet in height.

A few stories claim that the melonheads can communicate with each other telepathically, but for the most part, they're just humans with a mutated appearance.

Sometimes the melonheads are said to be more aggressive, throwing rocks at vehicles and chasing cars. There's even one story that claims that some melonheads stole a car.

These types of local legends often take on a life of their own as they spread around through the years, and getting to the root of the tale becomes more challenging over time. As for the origin of the melonhead, there are a couple of primary versions with a number of variations depending on location and who's telling the tale.

According to one story, back in the 1960s, a mental asylum in the area burned to the ground. All or most of the staff died in the fire as did many of the patients. A group of between 10-20 inmates escaped the blaze and fled into the woods. In some versions, the asylum's inmates set fire to the institution themselves as a way of escaping their imprisonment. Whatever the case, in the aftermath, the escapees stay hidden in the woods, not wanting to be sent back to their confinement.

Somehow, the inmates survived the harsh winter. Reportedly, they began to hunt whatever they could for food. This included wild game and people! Hikers, hunters, people simply passing by, basically anyone who came within the reach of the melonheads would purportedly vanish and end up…well…use your imagination.

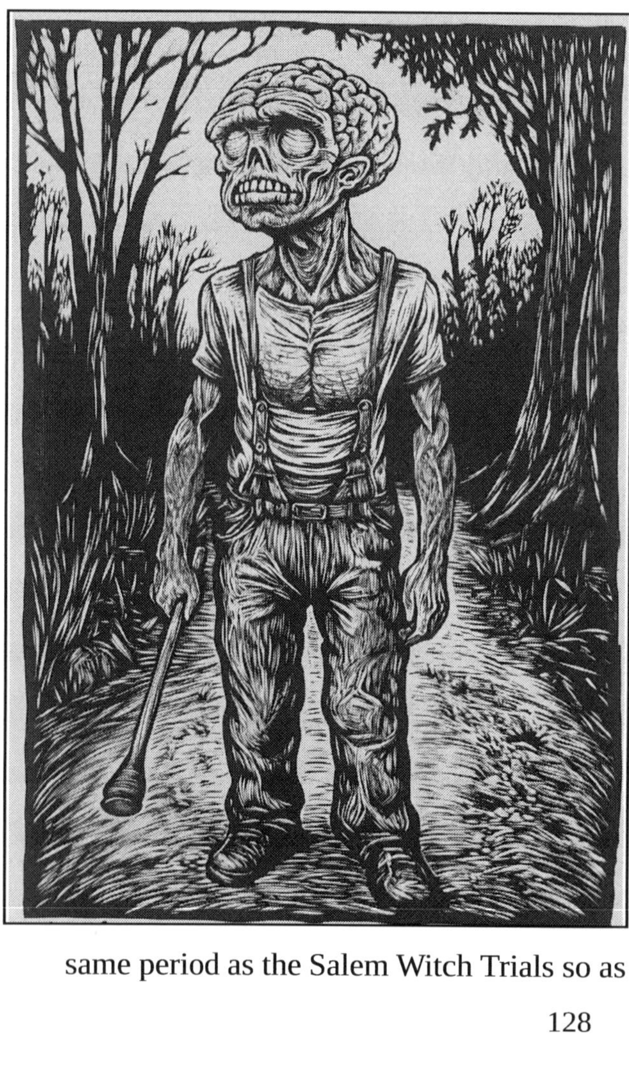

The inmates turned cannibals proceeded to inbreed and soon their offspring became disfigured in appearance leading to the large heads and other odd features that have become part of the standard description of a melonhead.

In some versions of the melonhead story, they aren't escapees at all, but simply a group of backwoods people who, after decades of inbreeding, have become disfigured.

According to another version, the legend of the melonheads has much older roots. This variation of the story begins in Colonial America when a family living in the Trumbull area was accused of being in league with the devil and practicing witchcraft. This occurred during the same period as the Salem Witch Trials so as you can imagine, the charges were a serious matter. The family didn't suffer the same fate as the accused in Salem, but the people of Trumbull did ban them from town. Cast out on their own, the family took up residence deep in the woods away from people, hiding probably for their own safety as much as anything else. Since no one in the community was allowed to interact with them, the family had to survive on their own. Over time they inbred and as the line continued, they became more and more deformed, eventually turning into what are now called the melonheads.

Most people think the entire tale, every version of it, is pure urban legend. The stories are certainly fantastic and have just the right blend of potential facts to make one wonder about the truth of the accounts. In looking at the melonhead tales, we have to consider whether there's any sustenance or history to any part of the stories.

The asylum version of the melonhead's origin has become connected to a couple of landmarks in the state. The now defunct Fairfield Hills State Mental Hospital and the Garner Correctional Institution, both located in Newton in Fairfield County, have been pointed to as possible locations that the melonheads escaped from. There's also a Federal Correctional Institution nearby in Danbury, so the traditionally rural area has played host to several correctional facilities and institutions. The Garner facility took in patients from the Fairfield Hospital when it shut and as a result, there were a number of adult male offenders with severe mental health issues at the facility. It's easy to see how the proximity of such individuals may have generated some fear—and tall tales—among the locals, and become a part of the melonhead lore.

There's an obvious theme of inbreeding running through various versions of the melonhead origin, but beyond this there is a medical condition that has been offered as a potential explanation for the melonheads. A birth defect called hydrocephalus causes large amounts of cerebrospinal fluid to become trapped inside the brain cavity. The result is that the individual's head swells and becomes larger than normal. Hydrocephalus can also impair mental development. If, at some point, an individual suffering from this condition was seen in one of the rural areas, it could have given rise to the legend, especially if this occurred in an earlier period when even fewer people understood such medical conditions.

There are a lot of purported melonhead roads in the state. They can reportedly be found along Edmonds Road in Oxford, Jeremy Swamp Road in Southbury, Downs Road in Hamden and Marginal Road in New Haven. They also purportedly lurk around various roads near Lake Mohegan and the Roosevelt State Forest in Stratford is supposed to be full of melonheads.

Boy Scouts on camping trips in Roosevelt State Forest have heard melonhead tales around the campfire for a long time.

Zion Hill Road, a possible lair of Melonheads

Ray Bendici, at the website *Damned Connecticut*, confirmed three particular melonhead roads: Zion Hill Road in Milford, Saw Mill City Road in Shelton, and Velvet Street aka Dracula Drive in Trumbull. Bendici notes that all three roads go through private neighborhoods.

Regardless of what town these big-headed beings show up in, the setting is always the same. A rural, secluded area with few to no houses around (save for broken down shacks the melonheads live in). The road, often dubbed "Melon Head Road" or "Dracula Drive," is typically a rustic lane, usually dirt, though over time, many of the classic sites have of course been paved.

A writer with the username "Doc" posted on the Damned Connecticut website on December 18, 2012, and reported:

"When I went to Stratford High ('78), it was an accepted fact that a family of melon head farmers lived on Dracula Drive (Velvet Road) on the Stratford/Trumbull border. It was a twisty road and there was only one house on it."

There's no doubt that decades of teenagers out looking for melonheads have added significantly to the legend. When I visited Dracula Drive back in the '90s, I spoke to a number of locals who recalled searching for the melonheads when they were in high school ten and twenty years prior.

Someone posting under the username "jello-buster" responded to an article about the melonheads posted on the Connecticut Live Journal Community website on November 22, 2005. He reports that he grew up in Trumbull and while attending Trumbull High School he visited melonhead road on many occasions. He writes:

"When I was a senior at THS we took girls down there and shut off our lights to get the girls to scream. I remember seeing one home on this dirt road up on a hill and they would have two large torches burning all night long, that was freaky! That was going back 13 years ago (circa 1992) but now I have a close friend that lives in the affluent town of Easton, CT, and to get there from Trumbull I can take Velvet Drive as a shortcut (only in the daytime!)."

The writer reports that most of the road is now paved except for portions which are part of the marshland preserve of Easton. "The freaky house still stands there on Dracula Drive," he notes.

With the legend being so widespread in the state, there are plenty of crossover tales, lots of confusion about what road is called Dracula Drive, and where and when the first melonhead stories started.

The muddling of urban lore, legend tripping, and teenage thrill seeking makes it difficult to come to a definite conclusion regarding the melonheads but it's just as curious to consider what makes the legend have such sticking power. While the melonheads aren't monsters per se, and they certainly aren't ghosts, they have a different appeal in terms of urban legend—they're close to human yet they're in an uncomfortable zone, one that makes them not quite human or normal. The escaped mental patient is unsettling and scary, but a person who is different because of inbreeding is there because of the breaking of a basic moral idea that disturbs people at a deep level. Combine this with the idea that the melonheads are cannibals, and we have a group of people who have broken yet another taboo.

These factors add a unique aspect to the legend of the melonheads, something beyond a "normal" swamp monster or wandering phantom. Perhaps, on some level, people are curious to see the melonheads because they wonder if someone really "went there" and became an inbred cannibal. Then, on the other hand, there is no doubt people who search for the melonheads just because they want an old-fashioned legend trip and thrill.

Whatever the case, if you happen to find your way on a lonely backroad in Connecticut, lock your doors and keep an eye out, just in case.

Resources and Works Consulted:

"The Melonheads Menace." Connecticut Live Journal, October 20, 2005.

Damned Connecticut website.

The Mysterious Outdoors

Hexenkopf: Pennsylvania's Witch Hill

By Kevin Lee Nelson

In eastern Pennsylvania old folk traditions live on, especially in Pennsylvania Dutch country. The term Pennsylvania Dutch is a bit of a misnomer, as the people are not actually Dutch. It's a misunderstanding by English speakers of the Pennsylvania German word "Deitsch," referring to the Pennsylvania German people in general, who are descendants of Germans who settled the area in the late 17th- and 18th-centuries. To English speakers the word "Deitsch" sounded like "Dutch," so the term stuck. The area is known for large Amish and Mennonite communities that hold on to old traditions and customs.

One of the traditions that has carried on into the 21st-century is the folk magic tradition of Powwow (called *Braucherei* in Pennsylvania German, which means, "to try"). It is one of a handful of distinctly American folk magic traditions that has managed to survive. Others include Appalachian Granny Magic, Hoodoo (not to be confused with Voodoo), Cajun Traiteurism, and Brujería. Many of these are hybrid magical systems that blend various European and Afro-Caribbean folk magic traditions with indigenous Native American magic practices and herbalism. Powwow is a healing tradition dating back to when America was a much more rural and isolated place. Trained doctors were far and few between, so people had to rely on traditional folk remedies when they or their livestock became sick or bewitched. When someone needed help they would often turn to a powwower or *braucher* to cure them. Traditionally powwowers never charge for their services, as they feel their abilities come from God, not the powwower. They believe that charging for something that is a gift from God is an insult to the Creator. There are still many practicing powwows in Pennsylvania and beyond today.

While Powwow is a healing, protective, and defensive tradition, what some people today call "white magic," its counterpart, *Hexerei* (meaning witchcraft or sorcery), is just the opposite. Hexerei is traditional witchcraft used to hex one's enemies and cause illness and misfortune — black magic. There are many tales of magical battles between powwowers and hexerei in Pennsylvania German lore.

One of the key locations in the powwow tradition is a hill in Williams Township in Northampton County called the *Hexenkopf* (meaning, "Witches' Head"). It got its name from the fact that the top of the jagged rocky outcropping has the profile of a withered witch's head. The location's name and reputation inspired generations of stories and urban legends of midnight witches' sabbaths held at the site, but the historical truth is it's part of a magical healing tradition.

The Hexenkopf is important to practitioners because it serves as a site for ritual deposit. Going all the way back to famous 18th-century powwowers like Johan Peter Saylor (1721-1803) and Jacob Willhelm (1744-1828), the Hexenkopf has been used to dispose of hexes removed from their patients. Many powwowers have specific specialties; some only treat burns or lacerations. Others only treat animals. But some specialize in removing hexes and combating hexerei. When someone practicing hexerei places a hex on someone it takes a powwower to remove it. The method of removing the curse depends on the type of hex. Once a powwower removes a hex they believe it doesn't just vanish and go away; it has to go somewhere, so traditionally they'd banish the hex to the Hexenkopf, believing that the rocky hill is remote enough and solid enough that banishing a hex there would not put anyone in danger. The belief is the hill will absorb the negative forces and neutralize them. One could look at it as a magical dumping ground for illnesses and curses. In Germany magical healers traditionally sent unwanted hexes to the peak of the Blockberg in the Harz mountain range in Northern Germany. So when settlers arrived in Pennsylvania, the Hexenkopf became their new waste management system.

As a student of powwow traditions, I naturally wanted to visit the Hexenkopf myself, considering its importance in the tradition, not to mention a considerable amount of fascinating folklore associated with it. On one of my trips to Pennsylvania Dutch country I met up with my good friend Patrick Donmoyer, director of the Pennsylvania German Cultural Heritage center at Kutztown University. He gave me a grand tour of the area's historic sites linked to the powwow tradition. Among these was a number of farms with beautiful barn stars, what many people call "hex signs," often associated with the powwow tradition. Some people believe they are magical wards to protect farms and livestock from hexes, but others feel they are just interesting folk art.

Along our road trip we also visited the grave of one of the region's earliest folk healers and powwowers known as Mountain Mary (circa 1749-1819), the medicine woman of the Oley Valley, and paid our respects. Some powwowers can trace their lineage all the way back to Mountain Mary. Interestingly, the art of powwow is always taught cross gender, meaning a man can only teach it to a woman, and a woman can only teach it to a man. The tradition's magical teachings have been passed down this way for centuries.

Barn stars, or hex signs

As the sun was getting low we concluded our tour by climbing the fabled Hexenkopf. The Hexenkopf summit is located at latitude 40.61778 and longitude 75,24167. At 820 feet above sea level it's one of the tallest peaks in Northampton County. The unique geology of the Hexenkopf has long intrigued geologists. It's made primarily of pre-Cambrian gneiss, a metamorphic rock formed by high temperatures. We made our way through the woods and climbed to the summit until the huge "witch's head" loomed beside us. It was truly an exhilarating feeling being at a location that is so steeped in magical lore. There are certain rare places around the nation that feel palpably different than the surrounding countryside. I'm not one to claim to sense "vibes" or "energies," but certain sites feel special; you can tell there is something different about it even if you can't say exactly why. The Hexenkopf is one of those places. A place where history, folklore, and magic all come together.

At the Hexenkoph

***Author's note — As I was writing this column a piece of Hexenkopf rock, that I keep on display on top of a bookcase, mysteriously fell off the bookcase, tumbled to the floor, and rolled over to me. Now THAT'S weird! It seems the Hexenkopf is making its presence known. Magic is afoot!

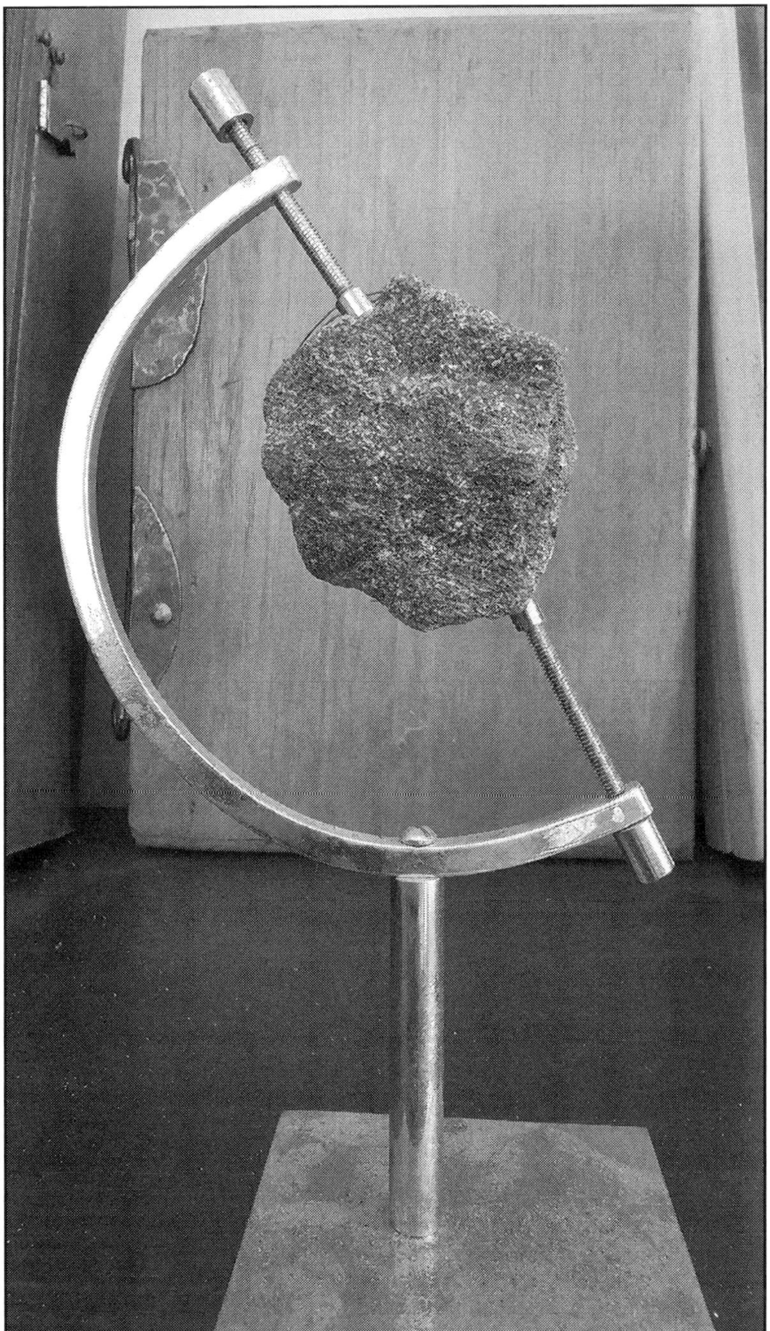

My chunk of the Hexenkopf

Resources and Works Consulted:

Bilardi, C. R. *The Red Church: The Art of Pennsylvania German Braucherei*. 2009.

Donmoymer, Patrick J. *Powwowing in Pennsylvania*. 2018.

Heindel, Neal D. *Hexenkopf: History, Healing, and Hexerei*. 2009.

Kriebel, David W. *Powwowing Among the Pennsylvania Dutch*. 2007.

White, Thomas. *Witches of Pennsylvania: Occult Mystery & Lore*. 2013.

I Dare You!

Visit a Crossroads on Halloween Night!

By: Chad Lewis

This bizarre dare is a tad bit different from the ones previously featured in this column due to the fact that this one is not at all bound to one specific town or city, or even a general region for that matter. This dare can be done anywhere throughout the country. This is the perfect type of dare for anyone with a strong sense of adventure because it combines several pieces of folklore that are absolutely spectacular on their own. However, when you combine them, the resulting dare morphs into one of my all-time favorites.

Let's start with Halloween night. Throughout history, many cultures believed that All Hallows' Eve was one of those special nights in which the veil between worlds is at its thinnest. This shrinking of whatever separates these realities means that we may be able to catch a glimpse of the unknown that lurks on the other side. Conversely, if we accept this theory, it means that whatever is obscured in the other world(s) gets a wonderful introduction to us as well. Since this night provides us with the best opportunity to cross realities, it only makes sense that it would be the ideal time to initiate rituals, dares, or soul transferring bargains.

Then we come to the crossroads portion of this dare. The folklore of crossroads plays an integral part in both the symbolic and literal belief in the power of the area. Crossroads are a fringe area where one is bound between spaces. In the literal sense, the danger, or opportunity of a crossroads, is that they provide you with the chance to create your own future based on how you decide to navigate them. They are also believed to exist in that liminal state between our world and the spirit world. Crossroads have always functioned as a paranormal ground zero. They served as the ideal location to bury the condemned souls of those who committed suicide and would not be allowed a proper burial inside the consecrated grounds of a graveyard. They were also the perfect dumping grounds for the forsaken bodies of murderers, rapists, and criminals.

In his wonderful research paper, *The Mystery of the Cross-Roads*, Martin Puhvel wrote this of the mysterious nature of crossroads, “In the recorded folklore of many lands, crossroads are associated with the appearance and activities of various, generally uncanny, creatures—ghosts, witches, and demons of many kinds.”

Any student of folklore will also recognize the most significant role of a crossroads as being the location for those who are seeking to sell their soul to the Devil. If you ever wanted to make a deal with the Devil, the deed would need to be done at a crossroads. The most infamous example of this unearthly contract was blues legend Robert Johnson. It is said that in the early 1900s Johnson sold his soul to the Devil in exchange for the mastery of playing the guitar. Being at a crossroads on Halloween night also provides any visitor suffering from a death wish with the perfect opportunity to try to summon a Hellhound. Even more difficult than calling forth these four-legged protectors of portals to Hell is keeping them under control because it is said that they will inevitably turn on their summoner-- resulting in deadly consequences.

Once the above-mentioned factors are taken into consideration, it is no wonder that it is said that anyone who visits a crossroads on Halloween night will be met with strange and eerie activity that often foretells of your future, including:

• If you are very quiet, you will hear the wind carrying the names of those who are about to meet their maker.

• Whatever problem is going to cause you the most consternation in the coming months will be revealed to you. The website americanfolklore.net expanded on this belief, writing, “If you go to a crossroads at Halloween and listen to the wind, you will learn all the most important things that will befall you during the next twelve months.” This strange premonition of the future is also believed to occur for anyone visiting a crossroads on Christmas night and New Year’s Eve.

Now, after considering all the above-mentioned folklore, I have decided that perhaps it was not very sensible for me to encourage you to take this dare. In fact, it might be downright dangerous advice. Instead of tempting fate at a crossroads, you may want to heed the countless warnings about crossroads that are littered throughout the folklore literature from around the world. No need to prematurely end your life when you could sit back and enjoy Halloween by watching all the trick-or-treaters---and don't worry, it is guaranteed that you will not get any tainted candy—well, almost guaranteed.

Resources and Works Consulted:

Puhvel, Martin. *The Mystery of the Cross-Roads. Folklore*. 1976, Vol. 87, No. 2.

www.americanfolklore.net

Disclaimer

The "I Dare You" column and its challenges are presented for educational and entertainment purposes only. The authors, publisher, and Back Roads Lore will not be liable for any injury to, or death of, any persons or for the damage to, or destruction or loss of any items or property, whether caused by gross negligence of the owners, its employees, agents, contractors, or any other persons, or for any other reasons associated with this publication.

Dedication

This issue of the journal is dedicated to:

Edgar Allan Poe (January 19, 1809—October 7, 1849)

American writer, poet and master of mystery and the macabre.

Born in Boston, Massachusetts, Edgar Allan Poe was the second child of actors David and Elizabeth "Eliza" Poe. His father left in 1810, and his mother died the following year and Edgar was taken in and raised by John and Frances Allan of Richmond, Virginia.

Poe is the first well-known American writer to earn his living by writing, a significant feat even by today's standards. Poe's dedication to the craft led to some difficult times in his life. He's considered the inventor of the detective fiction genre, and he had an influence on the emergence of science fiction as well. Even today, he is one of the most widely recognized American writers.

It seems somehow fitting that the man who wrote stories like the Masque of the Red Death and the Cask of Amontillado would have a strange end. On October 3, 1849, Edgar Allan Poe was discovered semiconscious in Baltimore. Poe was found by a man named Joseph W. Walker and taken to Washington Medical College for treatment.

Bizarrely, Poe was wearing clothes that were not his own. He was incoherent and could not explain what had happened to him. Prior to his death, he repeatedly called out the name "Reynolds," though no one knew whom he was referring to. The doctor who attended Poe reported that the man's final words were "Lord help my poor soul."

Not only was Poe's death mysterious, but in the aftermath, all of the relevant records related to his condition, treatment as well as his death certificate, were lost. Newspapers of the period reported that Poe died of "congestion of the brain," or "cerebral inflammation"; both were terms used for death due to "disreputable causes" such as alcoholism. No one really knows what Poe died from and the truth is likely to remain a mystery, a somehow fitting end to a curious and influential writer.

Back Roads Lore

Back Roads Lore began as a small collective of like-minded researchers with a simple mission—to chronicle anomalous events, Fortean mysteries, urban legends, and strange folklore. As the name implies, we put special emphasis on legends that are off the beaten track, but we don't shy away from high strangeness wherever it's found.

The individuals that are part of Back Roads Lore have put in decades of research and have traveled the world to unearth curious legends, but they don't rest! Exploring is an essential component of the work and with rare exception, we always make sure to visit the actual locations of the legends we investigate. One of the core tenets of Back Roads Lore is to get out there and experience these legendary and infamous places firsthand. It also allows us the opportunity to interview witnesses and locals and to better understand the perspectives of those personally affected by strange events. We aim to minimize so-called "armchair research," as there is no substitute for actual field experience and on-site observation. Such an approach also opens the door for countless adventures as we take deep dives into lost legends and weirdness.

It's not our goal to prove or disprove the existence of unusual creatures, cryptids, ghosts, aliens, or anything else. Rather, we prefer to present the facts, history, and lore, along with critical analysis, so that readers can make up their own mind and decide what they believe.

Amazing stories speak for themselves, but Back Roads Lore also examines new theories and unconventional concepts as we try to understand the deeper level of the strange events that happen in our world.

Lastly, many local legends and curious bits of regional lore are at risk of vanishing within a generation if they are not recorded and preserved. In the past, people kept unusual local tales alive mostly through oral traditions, often through storytelling at the local tavern or by passing strange cautionary tales down to their children.

Unfortunately, in today's highly mobile society and increasingly isolated culture, most people are generally unaware of the colorful and rich folklore of their own area. Unique history and folklore is something that should be documented and celebrated, as they play an important part of our cultural heritage.

Therefore, it is our hope that Back Roads Lore will fulfill a necessary role by discovering endangered lore and preserving it for future generations.

— Back Roads Lore

David Weatherly is known as the renaissance man of the strange and supernatural. Author, adventurer, magician and more, he has traveled the world in search of mysteries. From dusty castles to strange, remote islands and ancient sites, he has journeyed to the most unusual places on the globe seeking the unknown.

Kevin Lee Nelson is an author, researcher, and adventurer. He has written and lectured on topics of the paranormal, folklore, and the occult for over twenty years. A nomad at heart, Kevin spends much of his time roaming America's back roads in his black muscle car, hunting down strange legends and mysterious encounters.

Chad Lewis is an author, researcher, and lecturer on topics of the strange and unusual. With an academic background in the field of psychology, Chad has traveled the world in search of the supernatural. The more bizarre the legend is, the more likely you will find Chad there.

HALLOWEEN THRILLS...TRICK OF TREAT FUN
start at your nearest WOOLWORTH'S
Woolworth's Fabulous Fabric Costumes Fit Everybody ...And Every Budget!
Jet pilots to Pinocchio... Peter Rabbit to Indian chiefs and princesses... see Woolworth's collection of sweet-to-spooky masquerade magic! Sturdy fabrics, lavishly trimmed, in sizes for tots, teens and parents. Only a broomstick-ride away, at your neighborhood Woolworth's! With mask,
1.98 each
Black cats, clowns, pirates, devils . . . and many, many others. With mask, 1.49
Howdy Doody, Bugs Bunny, 'talking' Mickey Mouse and his famous Disney-land pals. With mask, 2.98
Jack-O'-Lanterns
Durable plastic. Light up when you insert flashlight bulb and battery! 3½", 29¢ 4½", 49¢ 6", 69¢
(Bulb, battery extra)
Halloween Masks Look Almost Real!
Delightful to fearsome, in vivid colors... wizardry from Woolworth's in a huge assortment of gauze and lightweight rubber masks! 10¢ to 79¢
Boxed Pops, Candy Bars
BUTTERFINGER, peanut butter, molasses. BABY RUTH, peanut butter, caramel centers. 12 big bars, 49¢ 40 miniature bars, 79¢
SAF-T-POPS. Hard-candy tops, no splinter handles. 80 pops, 79¢
Baby Ruth
Butterfinger
Tootsie Roll
Chocolate Tootsie Rolls
Twholesome twist-off pieces in each bar. 5¢ 6 bars, 25¢
'Midgee' Tootsie Rolls in bite-size pieces. Flavor-rich, individually wrapped. ½ lb. 25¢ 1 lb. 49¢
Manufactured by E. Rosen Company
Two-for-the-Money Treats...Halloween Toys With Delicious Pops!
Such fun! Plastic toys with cellophane-wrapped candies.
Horn blows! Complete with mask and pops 10¢
Pumpkin; witch-, cat-head handles. With pops 10¢
Witch and pops speed in space ship 10¢
Clarinet toots! Pops, candy dots included 29¢
Witch, pumpkin ride motorcycle with pops 39¢
At your nearest Woolworth store
F. W. WOOLWORTH CO.

Printed in Dunstable, United Kingdom

76896705R00091